DANTE

FOR BEGINNERS®

JOE LEE

Writers and Readers

Writers and Readers Publishing, Inc.
P.O. Box 461, Village Station, New York, NY 10014

Writers and Readers Ltd.
PO Box 29522, London N1 8FB
begin@writersandreaders.com

A Writers and Readers Documentary Comic Book
Copyright ©2001

ISBN 0-86316-280-0
1 2 3 4 5 6 7 8 9 0

Printed in Finland by WS Bookwell

Beginners Documentary Comic Books are published by Writers and Readers Publishing, Inc. Its trademark, consisting of the words "For Beginners, Writers and Readers Documentary Comic Books" and Writers and Readers logo, is registered in the U.S. Patent and Trademark Office and in other countries.

Publishing FOR BEGINNERS® books continuously since 1975

1975: Cuba • 1976: Marx • 1977: Lenin • 1978: Nuclear Power • 1979: Einstein • Freud • 1980: Mao Trotsky • 1981: Capitalism • 1982: Darwin • Economists • French Revolution • Marx's Kapital Food • Ecology • 1983: DNA • Ireland • 1984: London • Peace • Medicine • Orwell • Reagan • Nicaragua Black History • 1985: Marx's Diary • 1986: Zen • Psychiatry • Reich • Socialism • Computers Brecht • Elvis • 1988: Architecture • Sex • JFK • Virginia Woolf • 1990: Nietzsche • Plato Malcolm X • Judaism • 1991: WW II • Erotica • African History • 1992: Philosophy • Rainforests Miles Davis • Islam • Pan Africanism • 1993: Psychiatry • Black Women • Arabs & Israel • Freud 1994: Babies • Foucault • Heidegger • Hemingway • Classical Music • 1995: Jazz • Jewish Holocaust Health Care • Domestic Violence • Sartre • United Nations • Black Holocaust • Black Panthers Martial Arts • History of Clowns • 1996: Opera • Biology • Saussure • UNICEF • Kierkegaard Addiction & Recovery • I Ching • Buddha • Derrida • Chomsky • McLuhan • Jung • 1997: Lacan Shakespeare • Structuralism • Che • 1998: Fanon • Adler • U.S. Constitution • 1999: The Body Krishnamurti • English Language • Postmodernism • Scotland • Wales • Castaneda • Gestalt

This Book is Dedicated to Women,
Four:
My Dear Mother,
Jean Lee
The Librarian Who
Nurtured My Dreams,
Mrs. Mary Ropp,
My Aunt and Champion,
Dee Ann Russell
And Especially
My Beatrice,
My Wife,
Mary Bess Bohon Lee

"Vide Cor Tuum"
La Vita Nuova

CONTENTS

INTRODUCTION

✤ He had the face of the "Wicked Witch of the West," and, by some reports, the imperious disposition to match.

✤ He was a failed politician in his own city, and was exiled for his pains.

✤ He claimed a lifelong love for a woman with whom he may have exchanged only a few sentences, and more often then not, she treated him with disdain.

✤ He was born 700 years ago in a world fraught with petty but tragic intrigue, common brutality, and horrendous inquisition, all performed at the whim of both a church and state that met with his approval.

He was a poet whose greatest work was written in his own vulgar tongue, a language he believed would be made the common speech of an all-encompassing European Empire. It was finished almost literally on his deathbed, and could not have been read in its entirety during his lifetime, so why should anyone care to read it, or about him, now?

Why? Because he was **Dante Alighieri**, the greatest tourist (even if the tour was only a literary fantasy) this world and the next has ever known and, when one sees past the prurient and horribly satisfying grotesqueries of his sojourn in the inferno, he is, and will forever be the great poet, the prophet, the visionary champion of love.

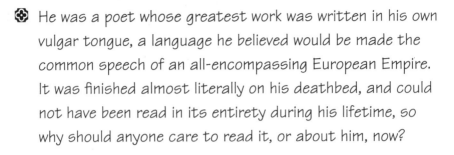

FLORENCE and the WORLD of the Late 13th Century

Love! Love is certainly the one thing that the world of 13th-century Europe could have used a little of. Let it be said that this was neither the best of times, nor the worst of times—it was a time of transition. Commerce was on the rise, pushing out the ancient regime: the feudal system. Wealth was becoming the standard of power, and those who claimed their titles from a higher power were none too pleased to have upstarts stinking of savvy and lucre taking over. This struggle was becoming particularly pointed in the northern half of Italy. Geographically Venetia, Tuscany, Lombardy, Emilia, Romagna, and the other regions were perfectly located as the crossroads of the trade between north and south, east and west. Cities like Venice that should have been nothing more than fever smitten backwaters were thriving, prospering bastions of the new capitalism.

No longer would populations depend on fertile farmland or abundant fisheries for their feed. Trade in silk, perfumes and every other commodity that might be desired could put ample quantities of food on the table. Smarts were becoming more important than mail-coated brawn. And those old hackers and slayers with tiaras on their brows and swords in their hands weren't about to stretch out on their gothic tombs just yet. The ironclad boys owned the land the caravans had to cross to get from city to city, and if you were carting goods on their roads, they demanded you pay their tolls, fees, and taxes.

The merchants balked, and where taxes pinch painfully in the wallet, death's fingers will not long be idle. The **Guelph** party was born to stay the miscreant hand of the **Ghibelline** nobs; thus city wars against city, party against party, and the gold and green landscape of northern Italy gets painted red with Latin blood.

The Ghibellines were eventually defeated for they, the noble landed class, had had their day and must now retire to the darkness of history. However, all was not exactly whoop-de-do for the Guelphs, as they had their own painful separation into two rival factions: the **Whites** and **Blacks**. The White party saw the papacy as a threat to their legitimate interests and thought Rome should be the seat of religious authority, and not temporal power. They longed for the return of the "Roman Empire".

The Blacks were not impressed with any romantic returns to "the purple" and thought rendering unto the pope was a better proposition than unto Caesar (as long as the pope was suitably reasonable in his request for rendering). So Black mixed it up with White and, lord, it all became a confusing shade of gray.

Florence was right smack in the center of all this turmoil, and even without this ongoing political folderol, the city had plenty of other problems to contend with. It had grown about three times larger in the 13th century than it had been in the preceding years, expanding far beyond the wall built during the Roman Empire.

New walls were eventually begun at the end of the century, taking fifty years to complete. Walls were very important for any polis at the time, because when visitors came to call, they often knocked with battering rams and rarely left with a cheery how-de-do. But the walls were also dangerous for what they kept inside.

Florence, so called for the abundance of flowers that grew there, was a steaming cauldron of pestilence and sewage, like any medieval city. Only the richest Florentines could afford that "modern" convenience: the cesspool. The rest must make do with dumping their chamber pots into the street, where errant pigs and dogs performed their work as sanitation engineers, and a good strong rain would hopefully rush it all into the river Arno, which burbled its way through the town.

Drinking water was dipped from public wells dotted through the various neighborhoods and not from the polluted waterway, but this "sanitary consideration" meant that when one's area drink went bad, everybody got sick. Is it any wonder that wine was not only considered a great revenant of the spirits but a miraculous panacea as well? (It is important to know that this was a time long before "germ theory" and microbiology. We humans looking for the causes of life conditions at the time had to postulate from information at hand. Sin made sense as the causal agent of plague and destruction when no other logic would answer, and witchcraft and devilment seemed likely suspects in the absence of verifiable sin.)

The houses were made of stone (a prevalent material in this mountainous region), when stone workers could be afforded. The richest, that swelling class of merchants and bankers, (the church's old proscriptions against money lending—it being a grave sin not to earn by the sweat of your brow—had finally fallen), were constructing grand palaces with tiled floors and tapestried walls.

The poor made do with hovels made from cast-off stone or easily secured wood, which was an extremely volatile material in a world warmed by open fires. Slum conflagrations were an ever-present danger. Streets were similarly economically distributed about the town with paved and guttered thoroughfares in the wealthy districts, and stretches of mud or dust (depending on the weather) in the poorer suburbs.

And humans is humans.

The church was the one place where every Florentine, or every baptized soul in Christendom, could come together in equal abundance and grandeur.

The well-to-do—men wearing the latest gaudy silk robes and women in *très chic* long-trained gowns balanced with a fetching *décolletage*, hair blonded by exposure to the sun in "blonding hats"—would rub shoulders with lice-ridden beggars (those little insects could also be spied cavorting between madam's exposed cleavage) in churches all over the city.

The beautiful baptistry of San Giovanni, and the monastery and church called La Badia still stand today, the Renaissance and other urban renewal projects having laid the others low.

The church was not only a building painted with frescos, jeweled with mosaics and lavished with gold. It was the center, the soul of the medieval world community. All were ultimately judged by its standards. If you managed to stave off the judgment in this life, you would undeniably be meted out your punishment in the next.

To stand outside the church meant not only excommunication from a religious body, but to place one's self against the workings of the natural world.

This is why the church in the early part of the 13th century, under the auspices of **Pope Innocent III**, launched a crusade against the **Cathars of Provence**. The Cathars, from the Greek word for "pure," were not some God-forsaken band of infidels in some far-off country. They were a Christian sect that had its roots in Gnostic tradition and not Roman Catholicism.

The Cathars—or Albigensians as they were also called because they were headquartered in the Provençal city of Albi—believed that one should bypass the dictates of a hierarchy and instead, concentrate on living a "perfected" life. The more perfect the life the more simple its demands, as matter was the creation of the devil and the spirit was trapped therein. The most perfected "perfects" actually starved themselves to death.

This was not the way to heaven according to the one, holy and apostolic church. Many people were converting to this heretical belief and the Catholic prelates and priests in the region were not only not combating it, but in some instances, they were embracing it. Pope Innocent said enough already, unfurled the red-cross banners, conscripted the troops (primarily the King of France, who was more than ready to annex this region as his own) and blew the charge. Provence would thereafter become part of France, a budding culture of art. The troubadours were primarily a Provençal creation, and tolerance was destroyed.

Dear Pope Innocent was politically shrewd, not just some iron-fisted bully. In 1223, after several years of cautious support, the **Franciscans** were incorporated as a new monastic order. **St. Francis** could easily have been seen as a heretic, sidestepping the usual ritual and urging his followers to live the life of Christ (instead of just insincerely mouthing prayers and buying indulgences), but inside the church, his message could be controlled and used to bolster the faith of the radicals who viewed the New Testament as a more important missive than a papal bull. The **Dominicans** were also founded about this time as an order of missionaries to the already baptized, to keep the faith approved by the shepherds of the flock, and not be pulled away by the "wolves" lurking at its edges.

But war, pestilence, squalor and death were not the sum total of medieval Florentine life. There was fun! Of course, death was part of the fun. Public executions like beheading muckety-mucks, burning heretics and POWs, and burying common criminals alive upside down in a hole were always diverting.

Horse races and gambling were popular pastimes that did not necessarily lead to bloodshed. Festivals, both religious and secular, were a time for singing, dancing and *jongleur*, acrobat and fool. Poetry was often a shared passion, with poets emulating the troubadours, demoting publicly and privately in witty and complicated rhyme. And of course, one must not forget the pleasures of love—not sex—as invented by the troubadours.

Love was the undying ember that burst forth in the breast and surely, eventually inflamed the entire being. Love was pure, not to be sullied by clutching fingers and spurting fluids. Love was not what a man held for his wife, as charming a companion as she may be, but for a blessed unassailable other.

Love, especially according to Dante (who was a bit more sympathetic to the carnal variety), was what made the world go round!

This world of love, hate and everything between was the world that Dante entered in 1265.

CHILDHOOD and YOUTH

On, or about, May 30th of 1265 in Florence a son was born to **Bella d'Alighieri** and **Alighiero di Bellincione d'Alighieri,**. They named him **Dante** and as his first biographer, **Giovanni Boccaccio** relates, his mother had a dream in which she delivered her son in a green meadow by the mouth of a crystal spring, directly beneath the branches of a laurel tree.

This tree of "poetry" dropped its berries between the lips of the gurgling infant and the most sublime lyrics issued forth. The boy, now a shepherd (things happen so quickly while visiting in the realm of Morpheus), stretched to pluck the leaves for his crown, misstepped, and fell down. No broken bones, but he transformed into a peacock, and flew off. Well, Dante's childhood wasn't exactly like that, but you can't fault a mom for dreaming.

Dante had the rather prosaic upbringing of any medieval urbanite. His father was a notary, a minor member of the legal profession entrusted with deeds, wills, contracts and his fellow citizens' little skirmishes with the powers that be. Both his parents were kin to families with more prominent social positions. His mother's distant family, in fact, had been driven into exile after an ancestor's treacherous deed, but she wasn't that related, so Florence was still her mailing address. Pop's family boasted the Crusader, **Cassiaguida degli Elisei,** who didn't quite make it to Jerusalem with the Second Crusade (of course, the crusade didn't quite make it either).

All in all, it was a pretty undistinguished childhood in his little house on the north side of the Torre di Badia. A little learning, a little adventure (he supposedly made like a boy scout and snatched another kid safe who was headed down for his third "full immersion" in one of the fonts at the baptistry of San Giovanni), and a lot of play. In fact, it was while attending a neighbor's party that his life took a decidedly different track.

SORRY, PADRE. I THINK WE SPILLED THE HOLY WATER.

BAPISTRY OF SAN GIOVANNI

DANTE'S HOME

May Day, 1274: the **Portinaris**, a very well-to-do family, were throwing their annual bash. Alighiero d'Alighieri took his son's hand and led him around the block to pay their respects to the big man himself, **Folco**. It never hurts to bow and scrape to your betters! The fiesta was in full swing. Adults and kids in their velvety best were dancing around the maypole.

Flowers grew, garlanded, bedecked the garden and all its denizens, but in that riot of bloom, Dante, like a bee to its nectar, had attention for only one: **Beatrice**, Folco's daughter, who was barely a year younger than Dante, born in April of 1266. So near, yet so far, Dante ached, "from that time onward, love was the lord of my soul". Wrapped in crimson, this pearl met him with an emerald gaze. No words were exchanged, but Dante had that gaze to recall for the next nine years, as he would not be in the presence of this rare blossom again until 1285.

Dante went back to his side of the block and proceeded to be a kid, but a little more serious than before. He grew more serious yet when his mother died in 1277 and maybe even more so when his father remarried in the next year or so. The senior Alighieri's new wife,

Lapa di Chiarissimo Cialuffi, in quick order provided Dante with some siblings, a lack he seemed not to have noticed before, and soon his seriousness was probably tinged with the certain displacement that the two new half sisters and brother brought as their birthright. It seems very likely though that Dante might not have had to suffer the pitter-patter of their little feet for long, and instead was regaled with the clippity-clop of hooves on the road to Bologna, the capital of higher learning, the seat of acquired European knowledge, the University.

No one knows for sure, but it has been suspected that Dante continued his studies in this august burg around the year 1279. He would have plowed his way through the Trivium—grammar, rhetoric and logic—planted his seed with the Quadrivium—arithmetic, geometry, astronomy and music—and after a short season in the sun, reaped the fruit of poetry. His cornucopia spilling, he returned to Florence, possibly upon the death of his father in 1282, to share his fruits.

A young man with a little money to burn, a roof over his head and a song in his heart, Dante quickly became the artiste of artistes. He traded verse with **Guido Cavalcanti**, an arrogant young knight with a nose wedged firmly in the air and a pretension of learning; **Manetto Portinari**, a fine young fellow with an even finer young sister (Bice, or more politely, Beatrice); **Forese Donati**, the sweet-tempered brother of Dante's future enemy, **Corso**; and all the while sharpening his gifts under the tutelage of **Brunetto Latini**.

Brunetto was widely known as a libertine, and even though Dante loved him and viewed him as the most civilized man in Florence, he would later see him in hell for his practices. This was a giddy time for Dante only partially caused by the great amounts of time he spent carousing.

It is not unusual for the serious boy to come back from university the sodden youth. But once again, a fateful meeting took place.

1283: Dante was in a rush, stepping across a bridge spanning the Arno. Beatrice was crossing from the other shore with two companions. The companions were beautiful, but beautiful as the moon to the radiance of Beatrice's sun. Love for this woman, whom he had not seen in nine years, dawned anew. The day spoke through Beatrice with such graciousness that the poet reeled with a blessed intoxication, and Dante was serious again.

COME ON ALREADY!

And he wrote, and wrote, and wrote. He wrote not of some idealized woman, some diaphanous metaphor for a grace and beauty unrealized. No, Beatrice was not exactly with him *per se*, but she did appear with him in his dreams, one of which he later set down in his book, **La Vita Nuova**: a flame-colored mist permeated his room, slowly a figure took solid form within the swirl, a figure of terrible beauty.

In his arms was curled a sleeping figure wrapped in a blood-colored cloth. Yes, it was she, Beatrice. Her bearer opened one hand to display a burning object and gravely intoned: "vide cor tuum," or "behold thy heart".

Next, he roused the slumbering woman and with a gentle but unrelenting pressure, forced her to take the heart between her lips and eat. Such a meal gave her no sustenance, but much fear and the angel, for it finally dawned on Dante that this was indeed the creature that bore his love, fell to grieving and leapt heavenward.

Dante awakened with raw anguish holding him in its unspeakable grip. Anguish and the suffusing power of love kept Dante asway for many years. A brief meeting with Beatrice would be followed with a sweet and tender lyric, one that would become popular in the streets of Florence.

Boccacio tells us that Dante was once traversing the work-a-day neighborhoods deep in thought when a voice broke through his mental occupation and stopped him in his tracks.

A blacksmith sang one of his most delicate poems, and, not knowing all the words, substituted some of his own.

Dante sprang into the shop and furiously began tossing tools about, leaving destruction in his wake. "Madman, what are you doing?" the smith implored of this fury. Dante blankly replied, "that is my poem you have mangled. You destroy my work, I destroy yours."

Message received.

NEXT TIME TRY THE ANVIL CHORUS.

Not all of Dante's encounters with the plebian classes were so high pitched, nor were his encounters with Beatrice, as fleeting as they always seemed to have been, as evocative of the most attainable reaches of love. To protect the privacy of his beloved, Dante often penned his missives to another woman. Beatrice was, needless to say, put out and was not shy to display her upset. Dante, of course, was quick to write another, less disguised work.

It was also about this time that both Dante and Beatrice were forced to pursue new careers: he as warrior and she as a wife. Beatrice was wed to a stolid young nobleman in the late 1280s, a match arranged by the parents since childhood.

This would certainly not in any way affect Dante's affections (as, has been previously stated, love and marriage were unwedded notions at this time, and a contractual obligation to one person did not negate the possibility of bliss with yet another). What did force a separation was war with the city of Arezzo.

The Ghibellines still held out in a few places, and one was Arezzo. Seizing control of the local government, they promptly tossed out all of the Guelphs, who ran to Florence, where the trumpet's clarion called all good Florentines to arms. It was 1289, Dante was twenty-four, and had yet to experience bloodshed organized on this level.

On June 11, Guelph and Ghibelline met at Campaldino. The Aretines charged under the command of their Bishop (clergy were allowed to fight and kill. They were proscribed from "drawing blood", however, and instead carried "hammers" and maces, not edged weapons). It was a fearsome maneuver, and pushed the Florentines back, but under the stern leadership of **Corso Donati**, they rallied and eventually took the day.

It was certainly not a day that Dante wished to re-live. From somewhere in the ranks, he hacked and slashed with the best of them, but he would later plunge those who fought for the sake of fighting into the pits of the inferno.

21

It was in the next year that Dante's soul was truly laid to waste by the ravages of war—not the war of man against man, but the never-ending battle of man against microbe.

On June 9, 1290, Beatrice, most fragile flower in the entire garden of Florence, became sick and she died shortly thereafter. Dante's anguished dream had proven portent of her fate.

"Depression" seems too mild a descriptor for the careening descent of Dante's spirit. "tears" too small to describe the bathing torrents that rushed from his life.

Eyes blinded, Dante grieved, and in his grief, he rediscovered the power of his art if not to heal, at the very least, to slow his fall and take account from where he had slipped and where he now stood.

This is **La Vita Nuova**, or *The New Life*, an autobiography. Dante takes the sonnets and canzones he had written thus far, and framed them with prose explanations of their origins.

It is from him we learn of his first meeting with Beatrice and their subsequent regard. It is from his specificity that we learn the corporeality of Beatrice is not to be questioned. She was decidedly not a poetic construct, but a living, breathing woman. And most importantly we learn that love, by its very nature, leads directly to the Divinity.

In 43 brief chapters, Dante sets forth his discovery, laying bare his artistic method in the process. First stirred by actual events, he distills the emotion of the happening down into one powerful idea. He then builds it up again into a lyric, but the poem itself then becomes as simple or as complex as one might be willing to enter. In fact, elsewhere in his writing, Dante is very careful to note that his work can be read in one of four ways:

(1) Literally ;(2) Allegorically; (3) Morally; (4) Mystically.

One could take, for example, the lines from the second sonnet (in Dante Gabriel Rossetti's translation):

Love (never, certes, for my worthless part, but of his own great heart),
Vouchsafed to me a life so calm and sweet
that oft I heard folk question as I went what such great gladness meant:
They spoke of it behind me in the street.

1. Love has made me so happy people stop and talk about it.

2. Love moves mysteriously through the world and even those deprived of it sense it in another.

3. Love brings joy undeserved but also its public burden.
4. Love, or rather, God's grace is impossible to comprehend but never goes unnoticed in the world.

Ultimately, *La Vita Nuova* is a chronicle of a man's love for a woman, and the grief that comes with her loss, a grief that transcends and transforms:

Beyond the sphere which spreads to widest space
  now soars the sigh that my heart sends above;
  a new perception born of grieving love guideth
  it upward the untrodden ways.
When it reached unto the end, and stays, it sees
  a lady round whom splendours move in homage;
  till, by the great light thereof, abashed, the pilgrim
  spirit stands at gaze.
It sees her such, that when it tells me this which it
  hath seen, I understand it not, it hath a speech so
  subtle and so fine.
And yet I know its voice within my thought often
  remembereth me of Beatrice; so that I understand it,
  ladies mine.

So goes the 25th and last sonnet of Dante's little book, which he ends with a prayer and a promise to continue the tale of his love and where it takes him at some future date. And does he ever continue!

ante's grief eventually muted to the persistent but dull ache that would allow him to get on with the business of living. Sometime in the 1290s, he married **Gemma Donati**, from a family that loved and hated him. It is likely that Dante and Gemma had been betrothed for years—a dowry certificate is dated 1277—in an arrangement by their families. Boccaccio can be blamed for the ugly rumor that Gemma could not compare with the beatific Beatrice, and was, in fact, a shrew and about as exciting as a dishrag. Who knows the truth?

Dante was certainly too much the "poet" to write about such mundane affairs, but Gemma seems to have been wife enough to give birth to a brood of little Alighieris. History is certain of three children, **Pietro**, **Jacopo** and **Beatrice**, and cocks a knowing eyebrow at **Giovanni**, who might have arrived sometime before the marriage vows. Whether because of discord at home or a need for something other than intellectual stimulation, Dante, in 1295, decided to fully enter the world of politics.

A VOTE FOR ME IS A VOTE OUT OF THE MIDDLE AGES.

Politics in 13th-century Florence (or really in any place at any time) was not the easiest thing to winnow out, and with all the machinations of the incredibly combative Florentines, it was very much like extracting Brer Rabbit from the briar patch. The city government was basically an extension of the **guilds**. The "major arts", as they considered themselves, were the **seven guilds** that elected the "Priors", the basic ruling body of Florence. With the "Podesta", an umpire selected from outside the city, the Priors had the difficult job of keeping life in the Polis running smoothly, or failing that, from running completely amok.

WOOL, NAH, TOO SCRATCHY.

The seven guilds included: the Judges and Notaries, the Wood Importers, the Weavers and Sellers of Domestic Wool, the Bankers and Money Changers, the Silk Merchants, the Physicians and Apothecaries, and the Skinners and Furriers. There were many other guilds as well—Blacksmiths, Butchers, Shoemakers, Woodworkers, etc.—but none commanded as much lucre as the majors.

The input of the other guilds was only sought on the biggest questions, when the **Council of One Hundred** was called.

WOOL GUILD IN FLORENCE

To get anywhere in politics, one must first join a guild. Dante surveyed the list, and being an intellectual and a poet didn't exactly qualify him for most of them, but he somehow decided that it made sense to join with the Physicians and Apothecaries. His way with words made him an ideal candidate for advancement, and it was very shortly after becoming a guildman that he was selected as ambassador to San Gimignano to help patch up a small dispute. Other small commissions followed, and Dante proved his skill at statecraft. His future in government for this moment was assured.

1300 was declared a year of Jubilee, and pilgrims who made the trek to Rome were to be granted special dispensations during this Centennial of the Birth of Christ. Dante took up the palmer's staff and made for the seat of Christendom in time for Easter Week. The city filled with devout souls, whose goal it was to reach the Basilica and seek the promised greater ease in the Afterlife. They prayed and took sacraments, but only Dante was visited with a vision, the "excessus mentis", the mystical transcendence of the consciousness beyond thought.

Dante was filled with light, one that would dim but never be extinguished, and that would lead him onward throughout the rest of his difficult life. But as there is light, there is also darkness and in Rome, living in the absolute pit of shadows was the Pope, **Boniface VIII**.

Cardinal Benedetto Gaetani was named successor to the Fisherman's Throne by **Celestine V**. This was an unusual move, as the College of Cardinals usually elected the new Pope after the old, but it was not completely without precedent. Many of the voices whispered that the selection was not wholly without coercion, and that Gaetani or one of his cohorts had whispered directly in the ailing Celestine's ear with a misleading angelic assertion that God himself wanted Benedetti's buns in the big seat.

Benedetto, crowned Boniface, was not exactly the logical choice for God to have made, for he, on many occasions, denied the Divinity's own existence and insulted many of the basic beliefs of Catholicism. God certainly does work in mysterious ways. What Boniface lacked in religious zeal, he more than made up for in the pursuit of Papal power.

For Boniface, the Church was decidedly the center of secular authority, damn the religious implications! Or rather, God must exist if only to assure Boniface of the existence of his Papal crown.

I MAY NOT BE MUCH OF A POPE BUT I'M SURE ONE HELLUVA POOP.

Boniface was not shy about his pursuits, and his expedient pacts with sundry other rulers were famous for their callous disregard of anything but the solidification of his own rule. His two most important papal bulls had exactly the same effect: the "Clerics Laicos" forbade any government to levy taxes against the clergy, and the "Unam Sanctam" unified all Christendom under the Pope's aegis. Dear Boniface, but for his emperor's new clothes, was naked in the face of the world.

Dante grew increasingly worried about Boniface's rapacious papacy and its plans for Florence. As the Pope sought more and more temporal power, Dante feared not only for the soul of Christendom, but for the specific spirit of Florence. Dante returned from the Jubilee with his head suffused in light, but not so bright that he could not discern its shadows.

In April of 1300, Dante was elected a Prior of Florence and if ever an election brought ambiguity to a man's life, it did so for Dante. Ever the cauldron, Florence boiled over. The Guelph factions of Black (Pro-Pope) and White (Pro-Emperor) heated the brew with a family vendetta, and watched or not, the bubbles weren't about to stop.

CERCHI HAS NO NOSE, SO HOW DOES HE SMELL? HA, HA, HA . . .

Corso Donati, arrogant champion of the Battle of Campaldino, was in negotiation with the Pope to bring the city under his control. The **Cerchi** family, staunch allies of Dante's friends, the **Cavalcantis**, wanted no strings being pulled in Rome to make them dance the tarantella, but on May Day the tarantula started the dance anyway. Both families were gathered to watch the spring festivities, and what began so innocently with a dainty skip amongst the flowers, ended with poor **Ricoverino de'Cerchi** without a nose on his face. Unfortunately, armed boys will be boys, and when a Donati takes a Cerchi nose, well, you can imagine.

With trouble in the streets escalating, Donati tried to push through a subsidy for **Charles II of Naples** (the Pope's fair-haired boy) in the priorate. "No way," the Priors voted. Maybe a little more blood in the streets would help. Finally in spring of 1301, something short of an all-out civil war had to be done. Toot-toodle-to, Dante to the rescue!

31

Dante had risen through the ranks of the priorate, being re-elected and then named **Commissioner of Public Works**. He was instrumental in calling the Council of One Hundred together in April. He succeeded in finding a solution to their immediate problem by making the streets safe. With the force of his righteous arguments, the Council voted to turn out the rascals: banishment for all those involved in the ongoing fracas.

It was a valiant and fair-minded stance on Dante's part, but it inflamed his enemies and alienated his friends. Among the exiles were foes like Corso Donati and beloved compatriots like Guido Cavalcanti (who would die before his return). In staking out the moral high ground, Dante would soon discover that ground exists only in rhetoric, and one who attempts to stand firm upon it will find his toes dangling in the air.

Rome was demanding an embassy. No one was better suited than Dante to go beak to beak with Boniface, but of course, going meant the Black faction would certainly play. Dante went off to Rome in October. While under the Pope's capacious thumb, he could only observe the entry of Charles II of Naples into Florence from afar. The Black faction and the seven Priors were victorious, and in January, Dante was banished from the city for two years and permanently excluded from office. No, wait, the Priors decided that wasn't bad enough. In March, Dante was exiled from Florence forever on pain of death. His journey had begun.

EXILE

*H*omeless, Dante would never again feel the comfort of his own four walls. For the rest of his life, he would have to rely, if not on the "kindness of strangers", at least on the kindness of benefactors who often had their own agendas.

The first was the **Conti Guidi** in Casentino. It was a short stay, and Dante made himself useful by heading an embassy to Verona, and then a visit to Forli. Back to Verona, Arezzo, Padua, on and on he traveled. Always a different host, a different cause to plead. He was, rarely, if ever, his own.

Dante referred to this period as the "darkening" point of his life. The rudderless time spent begging at other men's doors. One tale recounts a visit Dante made to a particularly wealthy and educated aristocrat. The poet arrived at mealtime, wearing his only clothing—dusty and road-

ravaged robes. The courteous nobleman immediately ordered
servants to take the tired rhymer by the hand and help him
into more suitable raiment. Dante returned in the finest of
14th-century finery, a veritable "clothe of gold" clothes-horse.
He took his place at the table.

Dante plunged his hands into tankard and tureen and proceeded to smear their contents over his borrowed fashion. His
host, no longer worried about delicate manners, bellowed for
an explanation. Dante tersely commented that it was obvious
from his treatment that these gaudy rags were intended as
the guest and not him. He only made sure the guest was fed.

Still, Dante was invited into hearth and home and, as much as exile rankled him, it also afforded him time to write, and write he did. Numerous letters, poems, and smaller works gushed from the fountain of his pen, but also longer, major opera burbled their way to the page: **De Vulgari Eloquentia** (*Concerning Common Speech*)—sometime from 1304-7—**Il Convivio** (*The Banquet*)—possibly 1308—and **De Monarchia** (*On Monarchy*)—1310. All roads, however, lead to the **Inferno** and it seems Dante was working on it at this time as well.

De Vulgari Eloquentia was probably written as a lecture for the University of Padua, or even his old alma mater, the University of Bologna. As the title indicates, it champions the eloquence of his native tongue, Italian. It is of course written in Latin (you gotta address such a defense to the intended academic audience after all). The work is divided into two parts.

The first is a history of language from the first words of Adam the Namer to the ill-fated architectural experiment of Nimrod, the Tower of Babel, and its subsequent crashing birth into the many homes of language.

It then looks at the particular babble of his native land and divides it into three separate groups: "oil," "oc", and "si" ("yes" to you.) And yes, it's all the same language, even if people got lotsa ways a-saying uh-huh. And, yes, Italian is a damn fine vernacular.

ciao

HEY, APPLE WAS MY WORD. WANNA BITE?

The second book continues his praise of his beloved tongue and then radically suggests that perhaps Italy, which doesn't yet exist—hint, hint, nudge, nudge—ought to drop all of the confusing dialects and speak one clear, expressive language. In fact, this "Italian" is already in use in the most sophisticated urban environs, it just needs a little standardization and then, with a little kick, everybody in the boot can be urbane, too. Come on, talk to me!

Il Convivio is literally a feast of learning. Chef Dante decided to finally serve up his little banquet in Italian. It was time somebody besides the boys in mortar boards got some nourishment. So come noble and commoner, man and woman, and grab a plate—its eatin' time. The meal was divided into four courses, treatises. Dante had originally planned fifteen treatises, but who can eat that much?

The *Convivo* is a similar mix to the *Vita Nuova*: verse as "meat" and prose as "bread", but this time the poet attacks

YUM, YUM, EAT 'EM UP !

the problems and meaning of love objectively, rather than subjectively. He uses the recipes of reason, primarily **Aristotle**, but also **Boethius**, the Middle Ages' great early philosopher. Boethius' book, ***The Consolation of Philosophy***, was written in a fifth-century prison. Its structure lends much to both the *Vita* and the *Convivio* with its interplay of verse and prose, but it is Boethius' view of philosophy symbolized as an idealized woman that struck Dante deeply.

So Dante postulated reason was to be viewed as the savior of man in this world as prison. With reason, one could anticipate divinity. With reason, one could discern true love, which descended from heaven and in turn represented the ladder of man's ascent. To be so informed created true nobility, and to be so ennobled filled one with spiritual grace, and with such grace one could truly live the happy life, no matter the conditions. Quite a mouthful, and certainly a sustaining meal for someone in Dante's unfortunate predicament.

De Monarchia represented the culmination of Dante's political musing. It seems likely that it was written in response to the election of **Henry VII** as Holy Roman Emperor in 1308. Dante saw this as the last best time to take his ideas on the issues of Church and state and disseminate them as widely as possible. He turned to Latin for his voice; his ideas being bigger than the whole boot of Italy.

De Monarchia is a tract advocating a one-world government as a solution to all political ills, and a paean to peace and prosperity. Taking Rome as his model, and the Pax Romana as the goal, Dante reasons that as God reigns supreme over all the entities that make up the universe so should one supreme power hold sway over all the various states and principalities of the Earth.

Rome did it once, so why not the Holy Roman Empire? One system of right and wrong to be administered justly—who

could complain? Well, the Holy Roman Catholic Church for one, for Dante envisioned a complete separation of Church and state: render unto Caesar, etcetera, etcetera! The Emperor must certainly bow to the Pope on matters of religion, God is still the Boss, but when it comes to the dust to dust stuff, the Emperor is the Man.

Dante got out the bunting in 1310 when Henry took a little trip, with a lot of clanking baggage, south to Italia. A few battles, a bit of persuasion at sword point, and even a stab at downright diplomacy. Things were looking pretty okay when Henry entered Rome in June of 1312, and got the nice gold hat plopped on his head. By Henry! This new world order just might be the thing after all. But no, Henry caught a bug, or rather, it caught him, and Henry died of a fever in 1313. No more Emperor. No more Empire. Dante folded his bunting forever.

There was only one thing for him to do—take a vacation. Somewhere no living soul had ever been before. No, not Pittsburgh, but a place he and W.C. Fields would both rather be.

The Inferno

Part I

*Midway in the journey of this life
I awakened to find myself lost in a dark wood
for I had strayed from the straight path...*

So begins Dante's **Comedy**. Comedy? One would be hard pressed to find any jokes in here, but comedy it is in the original sense, a tale that, no matter how tragic, has a happy ending. This comedy's a traveler's tale, a grand tour of places no living eyes are meant to see: the Afterlife.

In three books comprising 100 cantos (the **Inferno** has 34, because of its introductory canto, while both the **Purgatorio** and the **Paradiso** have 33) written in complicated **Terza Rima,** a rhyme that scans: aba, bcb, cdc, ded, etc., and in the vernacular Italian (a bold act of solidarity with both his ideas and his homeland), Dante lays bare the architecture of eternity in all of its awful and terrifying grandeur. The journey begins on Maundy Thursday in the year 1300, the year of the Jubilee. Dante turned the clock back to the time of his "excessus mentis", as well as his 35th year on the planet, a perfect point for a midlife crisis.

Holy Week is the most appropriate date for such a journey with its celebration of sin and redemption, death and resurrection. Medieval tradition also held that Christ had made a similar journey after his Crucifixion on Good Friday. "The Harrowing of Hell" was Jesus' reclamation of all the righteous souls who had anticipated, but could not lay claim to his salvation before the sacrifice on the Cross. All the holy characters that animate the Old Testament and a few New Testament figures, like John the Baptist and St. Joseph, finally got their one way escalator ride to Heaven. Dante's visit, however, for all its impossible blessing, was a voyeuristic one, and he could not, and certainly would not, claim any comparison to the Savior's.

Canto I

Lost in the dark wood, Dante stumbles and
falls his way on to a hill without trees.
Regaining his breath, he sets off
with at least the ability to
see where he's going. He
sees too much: a leopard
blocks his way. He turns. No solace
there, a lion. And then a she-wolf. These
three beasts have been viewed as symbols for
many different things, but all of them add up to sin.

John Ciardi perhaps offers the most satisfying explanation in his excellent translation: the leopard represents fraud, the lion violence, and
the wolf incontinence, the three
malignancies in which Hell is par-
titioned. Impossible to take the
high road (hint, hint). Dante
plunges back into the forest,
and almost into the arms of
a welcome figure.

I'VE NEVER
LOOKED GOOD
IN POLKA DOTS.

I MUSTA REALLY TAKEN A WRONG TURN THIS TIME.

The figure is none other than the Roman poet, **Virgil**, author of the Aeneid and, what a coincidence, Dante's favorite. Virgil is assuredly a ghost but an exceedingly friendly one, and offers our hero his services as a guide. Well, guide until he can go no further, only to be followed by another spirit (I wonder who?), who will take over the job of map reader.

Speaking of maps let's see where we are.

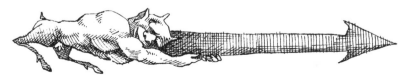

Imagine the inferno as a great, albeit oddly threaded, screw hole in the earth conveniently residing under Jerusalem:

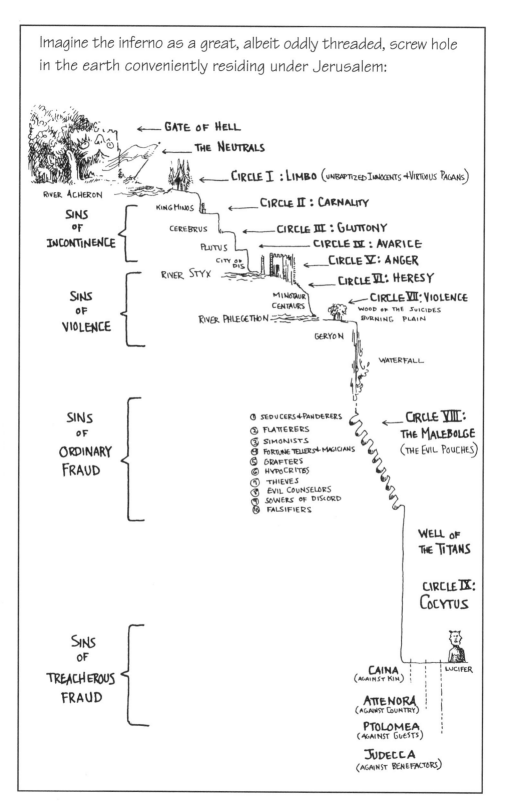

GATE OF HELL

THE NEUTRALS

CIRCLE I : LIMBO (UNBAPTIZED INNOCENTS + VIRTUOUS PAGANS)

RIVER ACHERON

KING MINOS

CIRCLE II : CARNALITY

SINS OF INCONTINENCE

CEREBRUS

CIRCLE III : GLUTTONY

PLUTUS

CIRCLE IV : AVARICE

CITY OF DIS

CIRCLE V : ANGER

RIVER STYX

CIRCLE VI : HERESY

MINOTAUR CENTAURS

CIRCLE VII : VIOLENCE

RIVER PHLEGETHON

WOOD OF THE SUICIDES BURNING PLAIN

SINS OF VIOLENCE

GERYON

WATERFALL

SINS OF ORDINARY FRAUD

① SEDUCERS + PANDERERS
② FLATTERERS
③ SIMONISTS
④ FORTUNE TELLERS + MAGICIANS
⑤ GRAFTERS
⑥ HYPOCRITES
⑦ THIEVES
⑧ EVIL COUNSELORS
⑨ SOWERS OF DISCORD
⑩ FALSIFIERS

CIRCLE VIII : THE MALEBOLGE (THE EVIL POUCHES)

WELL OF THE TITANS

CIRCLE IX : COCYTUS

SINS OF TREACHEROUS FRAUD

CAINA (AGAINST KIN)

LUCIFER

ATTENORA (AGAINST COUNTRY)

PTOLOMEA (AGAINST GUESTS)

JUDECCA (AGAINST BENEFACTORS)

THROUGH ME IS THE WAY TO THE CITY OF WOE
THROUGH ME IS THE WAY TO ETERNAL PAIN
THROUGH ME IS THE WAY OF THE DAMNED

ABANDON ALL HOPE YE WHO ENTER HERE

Canto II

Of course, standing within spittin' distance of the
entrance to Hell and having a ghost tell you that this
is the only way home may not be the greatest confidence
builder. Dante falters. After all, his knees played the
bone xylophone when confronting the beasties in the
woods—lions, and leopards, oh my! But what
about demons and unholy monsters?

AIN'T NO
DIRECTION
BUT THIS WAY

Virgil says he wasn't just out for a whistle
in the woods when he came across Dante.
No, **St. Lucia** had come to **Beatrice** in heaven
and told her of Dante's mortal peril: Beatrice,
filled with love, had descended to ask Virgil for
his services. That's all Dante needs: "I'm with
you, Lord and Master".

Canto III

"Abandon all hope ye who enter here..."

So reads the inscription over the Gate of Hell, the entrance
to the world of unending damnation. It is important to note
that for Dante, and for the Church as well, to be damned wasn't
the punishment for sin, per se. One damned oneself by turning

away from God. Sin could always be forgiven, but to arrogantly refuse to accept God—and to Dante, God is love—is to refuse to accept the natural order of the universe.

Rejection is damnation, and those who stand at this vestibule have already abandoned hope and love. A loveless world is hell. Only those who will to be there inhabit it.

Virgil senses Dante's dismay with this grim graffiti. It's easy to sense, for Dante has burst into tears. Virgil takes Dante's hand and pulls him towards his first steps into Hell. A dark plain. A vast multitude chases a red banner, buffeted this way and that by high winds. And to make the never-ending game more interesting, the souls are stung repeatedly by wasps and hornets. "These are they who could never make up their minds. Never good, never evil. Apathetic neutrals. Not worth looking at," Virgil says, and the two companions move past those who can't even get into Hell, to the great river, Acheron, the torrent that feeds all of the tributaries and swamps of the underworld. On the shore wait the dead, coins at the ready to pay the burning-eyed steersman, **Charon**, who will row them in his ferry to the nether shore.

"THIS BOAT IS ONLY FOR THE PAYING CUSTOMERS!"

"Get outta da boat," commands the captain, "you ain't dead." "Chill, Charon, what's willed, you can do," Virgil responds and whispers to Dante, "Charon is just wondering what a nice guy like you is doing in a place like this. Know what I mean?" Dante faints.

Canto IV

Thunder shakes the poet awake. He's made it across the river, and to the tippy-toed edge of the abyss. Nothing to see but roiling clouds. The thunder is none other than the gut-churning cries of those unseen below.

Virgil leads Dante into the first circle of Hell, **Limbo**, where he resides. No more crying here, but the air trembles with sighs, not because of the pain of punishment, but for the detachment from God. The place is peopled with all of the virtuous pagans, ignorant of Christ, and all the children who never got to be introduced through baptism. Not a bad place, but not heaven.

It was from here that Christ brought up the chosen, Jews, both patriarch and commoner, on Holy Saturday.

But not even the opportunity of a chat with **Socrates** or **Saladin** can stay their journey.

FOR THIS I GAVE UP ORGIES?

Canto V

They descend into the darkness of the second circle: The **Circle of Judgment. Minos** sits grinning. Every confessing sinner comes to him to be weighed. "Hmmm. Heavy as a blasphemer." He winds his snaky tail around his gut to correspond with the circle's number that suits the crime, and snap! Out they fly into the pit.

Minos is none too happy about not getting the chance to pitch Dante, but hey he ain't got no say. There are those not far flung that, like some crazed flock of birds, wheel and wheel directly above them. They are the **lustful**, and the heat of their undying and unfulfilling passion keeps them forever aloft. **Cleopatra**, **Dido**, **Achilles**, and **Tristan** are all there, and Dante spies a sad young couple, and calls out to them.

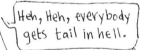

Heh, Heh, everybody gets tail in hell.

They are **Francesca di Rimini** and **Paolo Malatesta**, her lover and brother-in-law. She was married to **Gianciotto**, a cruel and hideous fellow, whose greatest crime was inattention, so his little brother stepped in to fill the breech. They were eventually found out while reading the sinful exploits of Lancelot and Guinevere, no less. And as Francesca sweetly says, "We read no more that day".

Dante hits the dirt in a swoon again.

Canto VI

This time Dante enters the third circle, the **Circle of the Gluttons**. The bloated bodies of sinners lie over the landscape. Too fat to move, they are pelted with a never-ending rain of ice, hail and filth. **Cerberus**, the monstrous three-headed dog of mythology, cruelly keeps his watch, occasionally breaking for a bit of fresh human flesh—hey, he's eating for three.

As the poets pick their way across the squealing pavement they are accosted by **Ciacco**, (the pig) a Florentine of Dante's acquaintance. Here we join Dante and learn that the dead have complete foreknowledge of the doings of their still quick compatriots. Because Dante cleverly sets the narrative slightly in the past, he can have characters accurately predict the inevitable future. Ciacco does so. He tells of Florence's division and Dante's exile. Old news is still painful news. Ciacco falls back into the stupor of his torment and, with no more to hear, the two move to the downward egress of the next round, where they are assaulted by **Plutus**, a.k.a. the great enemy.

Canto VII

"Papa Satan, Papa, Aleppe."
Plutus screeches in rage. No one
can figure out what Plutus is on
about as "Aleppe" is a completely
unknown word. Of course, no one
is quite sure if Plutus is meant to
be Pluto, Roman god of the underworld, or Plutus, god of wealth, who by all
other accounts isn't such a bad guy to meet. Plutus would
be a likely choice as they are now entering the fourth circle
where **avarice** is punished.

Virgil responds with a curse invoking the archangel Michael
and Plutus, the old wind bag, collapses like an empty purse.
Virgil certainly has a way with these bogies—something to
look for in a guide through Hell. Now the poets can see the
rush of avarice clearly. And rush it is, with two great armies
of shades pushing huge boulders into each other. In this cor-
ner we have the hoarders, and in the other, the squanderers.
Their faces are indistinguishable, as the blindness of acquisition has rendered them featureless. However, one thing is
evident: many are obviously clergy, as they still have their
distinctive tonsure haircut.

Yeah, but
mine is
still bigger
than yours.

Virgil and Dante move on to the fifth circle: **Anger**. This is a wet circle. A stream flows making the earth a sponge of mud and filth. Constant warfare is carried on in the **Styx**, a marsh where they witness a nasty biting, tearing, eye-gouging species of mud wrestling, carried on for no other reason than everyone is forever pissed. The **Wrathful**'s footing is made even more treacherous by the sullen writhing and kicking beneath their feet, sunk forever in the gloomy misery of inaction.

Inaction isn't the way of our boys. They carefully pick their way through the slime to a high tower in the center of the mess.

Canto VIII

A flame erupts from the tower only to be answered by another flame across the morass. One, if by sea, one if by **Phlegyas** it seems. Phlegyas is one more disgruntled ferryman

HEY, WATCH IT! I'M BEING PUNISHED DOWN HERE.

unwillingly pressed into becoming the taxi of the damned. Cab service isn't so easy in the Styx, with hands and feet constantly trying to gain purchase over the gunwalls, and those angry souls trying to "Rock the boat, Baby".

Dante starts. He recognizes the filth-disfigured face of **Filippo Argenti**, a most arrogant and disruptive Florentine. Phlegyas gives him a good paddle, and Dante is none too upset to see his ugly carcass splash back into the ooze.

Slowly, through the stagnant air, they can discern red walls glowing like heated iron. Along the tops sit fallen angels as annoying as Hell's pigeons. They disembark before the forbidding palisade. The pigeons refuse to open the coop to the City of Dis.

COME ON HAVE A HEART.
LEMME IN THE BOAT.
IF I COULD WALK
ON WATER, I WOULDN'T
BE HANGIN' HERE
WOULD I ?

Canto IX

Things are looking bad. Virgil is unable to get them to open the gates. The **Erinnyes**, the furies, arrive making things worse. As their snaky locks writhe and thrust to quench their thirst with blood, the angry bat-winged hags scream for the aid of their cousin, **Medusa**, to turn the poets into stone.

Virgil is worried, and lovingly covers Dante's eyes with his own hands, knowing that there exists evil that no man can see. At this darkest moment, hope arrives. A wind, scattering the angry like frogs in a pond, sweeps forward and in its breast resides an angel (with its allegiance still intact). The heavenly being shoos its debased siblings back, and the gates swing open. The poets enter **Dis**, a city of flaming tombs.

Canto X

This is the sixth circle: the cemetery of the **heretics**. Here languished all those who tried to subvert God's master plan by professing every ridiculous wriggle and strike counter to his revealed word. Flames belched out of every sarcophagus, burial wasn't enough of a punishment for these damned ideas. They must be roasted as well.

One soul jack-in-the-boxes out of his enclosure as he catches Dante's Tuscan accent. It's none other than **Farinata**, the Ghibelline war-chief, and Dante's pal, Guido Cavalcanti's father-in-law. Not to be left our of the conversation, Guido's old man, *Cavalcante*, pops out of the toaster asking for news of his boy. This is one of the stranger features of Hell, as its inmates have complete knowledge of the future, but they lack any inkling of the present. They are suspended in perpetual ignorance of time passing. Cavalcante, ever the doting papa, insists his boy is the best scribbler of them all, and should be doing this journey. Dante clams up and senior faints away thinking his junior must be dead if he's too busy to visit his sire. Farinata, so self-possessed he's oblivious to the flames, prophesies more of Dante's eventual misfortune. You don't go to Hell lookin' for a good word.

MY BOY'S BETTER THAN YOU BOY.

Canto XI

Virgil and Dante continue onward through the heretics' graveyard. Noticing the growing disarray of stones, the old Roman explains that the wreckage was caused by the earthquake that shook both Heaven and Earth at Christ's demise. At the edge of the Seventh Circle, they are repulsed by the stench emanating from below. While acclimating both breath and stomach, Virgil explains the Aristotlian nature of the inferno. Old pagan that he was, Aristotle discerned in his

Ethics the divine order of punishment. The incontinent sins—lust, gluttony, greed, are bad enough but they don't compare in severity with violence and fraud, which are located within the city of Dis. **Treachery** is by far the worst case of fraud, and accordingly, its practitioners reside in the deepest Hell. Dante clicks on everything but usury, money-lending. Virgil explains that usury, the acquisition of wealth from wealth and not from work, is a sin against the natural order, and what is against nature is against God. Seems Dante wouldn't exactly be happy on Wall Street does it? But maybe Wall Street is located a little farther downtown than we imagined.

Canto XII

The poets carefully climb through the jumble of stones until directly in the downward cleft, they meet the **Minotaur**. This "infamy of Crete," the issue of the unnatural union of a divine bull and a mooing human queen mistakes Dante for his nemesis, **Theseus**. In a rage of psychotic violence, the bull-headed beast tears his own flesh. Virgil, no mean psychologist, correctly sees this as a manifestation of the monster's inward rage and with a few choice words (a very effective talking cure) skedaddles old horny away.

The seventh circle, the realm of the **Violent**, is het-up with the muy famoso creatures of myth. **Centaurs** roam the shores of the river **Phlegethon**, a river of boiling blood that rings the entire circle, keeping the drowning swimmers in. The swimmers—tyrants and murderers—are quite a distinguished lot, including both **Alexander the Great** and the not so honey, **Attila**. The Centaurs themselves are no shabby crew with **Chiron**, Hercules' mentor, holding the reins of command and **Nessus**, Hercules' outfitter (it was the flesh-burning cloak of his hide that convinced Mr. Universe to hike it to Olympus), serving as taxi across the bubbling waves.

COME ON. NO FARES AIN'T FAIR.

Canto XIII

On the other side, the travelers
enter a forest that one decidedly, un-
blindingly can see for the trees. The trees are
the tormented souls of the **suicides**, and in
their aching branches nest their chief tormen-
tors, the **Harpies**. These hybrid abominations, both
vulture and human, feed on the leaves and branches of those who did the ultimate violence to
themselves. And when the bough breaks, the baby
will bleed, which gives them voice, so they hear
the sad tale of **Pier della Vigna**. Della Vigna,
much like Dante himself, was a poet, philosopher and a champion of lay authority. It was
this later capacity that recommended him as
councilor to **Frederick II**, the Holy Roman Emperor
and father of Dante's hope, Henry. High-mindedness,
clarity of purpose and honesty are often impedi-
ments to the ambitions of unscrupulous bureaucrats,
so to ease their upward climb, they accused Pier, their
stumbling block, of treason. In despair, the poet committed the greatest injustice to himself.

A terrible race interrupts, crashing and tearing
through the underbrush. These are the **Wasters**, those
who inflicted violence upon themselves by throwing
away what they graciously received, and they are
forever pursued by wild and ravenous dogs. The slow
unwillingly give a hot lunch to the pups. Everyone
slows at some point.

Canto XIV

As they carefully make their way out of the dismal wood, Dante stops to compassionately re-attach some leaves to the bush with whom they have been talking. They come to a broad wasteland, a desert of burning sand constantly assaulted by a rain of fire. The denizens of this sterile (sterile because this is the place for sins that produce nothing) plain are people who did violence to God, art and nature. The **Blasphemers** lie spread-eagled with every inch of their being basted from above or below. The **Usurers**, their sin being slightly less, are allowed to sit. The **Sodomites** are allowed to hot-foot it across the sands, but never fast enough to dodge the licks of flame.

Dante and Virgil skip lightly until they reach a small bloody trickle of the Phlegethon, and Virgil explains the origin of the many rivers of Hell. It seems that enclosed in Mount Ida on Crete stands a statue with shoulders toward the east and face turned toward Rome searching for reflection. Its head is gold, torso and crotch of brass, legs fashioned from iron and, bearing the brunt of his weight, the right foot is made of clay. This icon of the ages of man is pierced with fissures in every part but the fine gold head, and from these drop tears, which collect and form the ever-descending rivers of the inferno. They freeze in the deepest pit of Cocytus and from there, as if redeemed, flows the river of forgetting, the **Lethe**, that courses through Purgatory.

JESUS, IT WAS ONLY A LITTLE BLASPHEME!

Canto XV

The poets find that, as they continue along the sanguine stream, they are afforded an over-hanging shelter from the fiery storm. A group of Sodomites comes jogging by, and one, in disregard of his torment, stops and hails Dante. Dante is able to recognize his beloved mentor, **Brunetto Latini**, through the sad, scorched visage. Tenderly, and with unmasked affection, the two speak to each other. Brunetto engages in some of the bitter prophecy that is now all too familiar, but he also offers words of the kindest encouragement:

> "If you follow your star
> you will not fail to find your Heaven..."

and sage advice:

> "He who listens well takes note of what he's heard."

And with a farewell, for Hell waits for no one, Brunetto asks only that his treasure, his work, the *Livres dou Tresor* and the *Tesoretto*, be remembered fondly, the only kind of sweet immortality left to him.

I STILL SAY Ta-MÄ´TŌ.

I DON'T THINK IT'LL FLY.

Canto XVI

As the poets get closer to the edge of the seventh circle, the roar of falling water grows louder and louder. The Phlegethon must splash to a considerable distance below. Contemplating the next adventure to come, Dante, by the distinctive Florentine cut of his clothes, is recognized by three more Sodomites, all illustrious former members of Florence's upper echelons. **Guido Guerra, Tegghiaio Aldobrandi** and **Jacopo Rusticucci** were all wise and highly esteemed men in their lifetimes. All request news of the old hometown. Dante obliges with his tale of woe.

It is interesting to note the number of friends and acquaintances Dante has in Hell (he will certainly not be completely anonymous in the other environs of the Afterlife) and even more worthy of note, how he treats them. For some he displays his utter and total contempt, not a surprising way to treat the damned after all, but quite a few, he treats with warmth and compassion. Dante chooses not to turn his back on those who have turned their backs on God.

At last, they come to the precipice, and its descent creates a formidable problem for our tourists, unless Virgil resolves such imbroglios. He asks Dante for the cord wrapped about his waist—a cord that has been the subject of much scholarly speculation (like what is Dante doing with a rope tying his pants up, anyway? Does this mean he has some ties to the Franciscan order? Or maybe enjoyed entertaining with lasso tricks long before Will Rogers? I think he was just a "be prepared" sort of guy and probably had a pocket knife too!). Virgil dangles it over the edge and above them flaps a grotesque figure.

Canto XVII

The figure is **Geryon**, the master of fraud. He is the only way down to the next circle, and it's going to be a bumpy ride. Hercules dispatched Geryon here. He has the wings of a falcon, the head of a man, a reptile's body, shaggy animal claws, a tail with a scorpion's sting, and to unify the whole crazy quilt of a creature, flashes about every color under the sun. Virgil needs a bit of privacy to negotiate their passage, and urges Dante to take a look at the **Usurers**, those who do violence to art.

They hop about the sand with asses scorched by the silica, heads burnt by the sky. Tears perpetually pour from their eyes, the only recognizable feature left in their debased faces, blurring the sight of their big fat purses, those anchors that pulled them below. Each purse is painted with their family crest, some Florentine, but these are a bunch of sinners Dante doesn't know. Time to saddle up and head south. A slow, dizzying descent with not a drop of Dramamine, and Dante keeps his eyes squeezed tight, happy to set his feet firmly in Hell yet again.

Canto XVIII

Dante must not have had his eyes closed that tight because he was able to get a glimpse of the landscape below. This is the eighth circle, where "ordinary" **fraud** is punished. This circle is called the **Malebolge**, the "evil pockets". Each pocket or trench is a deep concentric ring where fraud meets its just desserts. One must cross a system of bridges to get to the edge of the "Well of Giants" and down to the deepest Hell of all.

The first pocket is reserved for seducers and panderers, pimps to us. These two classes of sinners are forced in two files on either side of the foul ditch to forever march. Their lines are kept straight and their steps lively by whip-lashing demons. That's right, demons, the horned, spiky-tailed fellows that we expect to see in the inferno. Finally, a few of this crew are recognized with ancient **Jason** chief amongst them—he who did the nasty with **Hipsipyle**, and then with the sweet mother of his sons, **Medea**. Dante also gets a dig in to old Bologna, which has provided more than its share of inhabitants to this ditch.

The second pocket represents the grossest of all Hell's punishments. **Flattery** will certainly get you somewhere—in deep doo-doo. Here those who sought to gain by golden tongues have the bell of their mouths forever silenced. You can't scream with a mouthful of shit. Below, they drown in a turgid river of excrement.

GET ALONG LITTLE SINNERS

COME ON IN THE SHIT IS FINE.

Canto XIX

The third pocket, which the poets now cross over is reserved for a sin that particularly raises Dante's ire, the sin of **simony**, which we today would call the tele-evangelist's sin. It was named for **Simon Magus** a not-so-good Samaritan who tried to purchase spiritual power from **Simon Peter** with a few greasy shekels. Failing that, he challenged St. Pete to a contest of magic feats. Magus flapped into the air. He should have stayed in the bush, for Peter tossed a prayer in his direction and down came Simon Magus. In this bolgia, those who traded in indulgences and ecclesiastical offices were dropped head-first into holes in the ground. Exposed only from knees to feet, their soles are constantly basted by oily flames. The brighter the flame, the bigger the game.

Dante stops at the biggest fire and asks Virgil to help him down into the trough. Virgil gathers Dante in his arms and carries him like a child. Flambeau feet is none other than Pope **Nicholas III**, and while he recounts his numerous crimes, he lets slip that his successors, Pope **Boniface VIII** (Dante's old nemesis, who was certainly roasting in Hell even as Dante scribbled) and **Clement V** would soon be joining him. In that there was only a finite number of holes and a seemingly infinite number of simonists, new arrivals would smack into the top dog and slam the ones beneath deeper into the burrow. Dante likens the ugly punishment to a reverse baptism—most un-Catholic in its eventual full emergence. After Nick suffers a little chastisement from Mr. Alighieri, Virgil takes the poet to his breast and upsy-daisy.

Canto XX

Now Virgil and Dante, by way of a rock bridge, cross the fourth pouch, the assigned place of punishment for **diviners**, **astrologers** and all those too impatient to let the future naturally turn into the present. They are a sorry and miserable lot. Eternally weeping in their endless march around the ring, their tears don't soak their breasts. No way, their tears flow over backs and drip down to the cleft of their buttocks. For their bizarre attempts at forecasting, they are all doomed never again to see before them. Their heads are twisted around to face the rear, and their feet move, bouncing and jouncing, forward.

Many whose names have been lost to history stumble here. A few like **Tiresius the Theban**, acquaintance of **Oedipus**, and his daughter, **Manto**, are still remembered. In fact, Manto, by virtue of having died there, is the unwitting foundress of Virgil's native city, Mantua. The poets, sensing the moon's set and sun's rise, hurry on for all those seers don't really have much to see.

IF YOU COULD SEE WHAT I SEE...

Canto XXI

The fifth *bolgia* awaited those who committed the sin of **barrotry**, graft—the selling of political favors. It is a place of boiling pitch watched over by the viciously hilarious **Malebranche**, the "evil claw" demons, some more rootin' tootin' (and I do mean tootin') devils.

As the two versifiers stand, a demon comes swooping in and tosses a senator from Lucca headlong into the bubbling ooze. The rules are succinctly explained to the newly damned politician. "You poke outta da pitch, we pitchfork you back into da poke." And these coal black devils mean what they say; their salad forks can do some damage. It seems they fork an inordinate number of Luccans. Remember, Washington, D.C. had yet to be founded.

Finding the footbridge collapsed into the stew, Virgil tells Dante to hang back a bit while he goes off to ask directions from **Malacoda**, "evil tail", the leader of the crew. Malacoda takes a bit of persuading but succumbs to Virgil's higher mission. Dante, a living man, is a rare sight for these keepers of the graftful dead and they itch to test their instruments on his backside. Malacoda not only puts the word on them but also conscripts a group of ten to provide an honor guard. They aren't exactly Santa's reindeer. There's Alichino and Calcabrina, Cagnazzo, Barbariccia, Libicocco, Draghignazzo, Ciriatio, Graffiacane, Farfarello and Rubicante. Their names are mostly non-sense. Barbariccia is "curly beard", Draghignazzo is "big dragon", Graffiacane is "dog scratcher", and Rubicante, "red changer", but this is one serious pack of fiends.

Assembled and ready to roll, they salute their captain: a pointed tongue stuck straight from their mouths. The captain signals, as Dante put it, "he made a trumpet of his ass."

Canto XXII

They continue with their "merry" companions who remain ever vigilant for sinners who dare to ease more than a "frog-muzzle" out of the hellish slime. Graffiacane spies one easing more than a snout into the smoky air. He pulls him out, and the demons, like cats to a mouse, begin to "play". Captain **Barbariccia** will have none of it, and lets Virgil try a little interrogation. He's a servant of **King Thibault of Navarre** and keeps talking despite the occasional pig tusks of Ciriatio or the hook of Libicocco. The prospect of a few puffs of this foul air, and a respite from the burning pitch and the chatter of his fellow Sardinian inmates is just too good to pass up. Ah, but even this must end, and a little demonic rippin' up begin.

The barrator suggests a wee deal. How's about more sinners to torture than just little old him? Hmmm? He would
just give a little call, and out they would pop like otters and
then… Alichino assents, why not? The sneaky Navarrese
crouches from his "hallo" and swan dives into the deep instead.

Alichino is pissed, and Calcabrina is pissed at him and his
folly. They set to in a dogfight over the brew. Fang, tail and
claw, they fall in. Their brother devils give up their guidance to
try to hook the scorched duo back to shore.

DEVILS WILL
BE DEVILS.

Canto XXIII

When the Malebranche fish their brethren from the pond, they will be in need of a little sport. "Let's move" is the poet's silent cry. Virgil takes Dante as "a mother takes her child", down the steep bank of the sixth *bolgia*, the place of the **Hypocrites**. There they march in gloriously gilt robes, in the shape of monk's habits, but the gold hides the true leaden garments of their sin and with its weight they must endure.

Two of the inhabitants of their gilded cages were members of the order of the Glorious Mary, a.k.a. the **Jovial Friars**. These monks began their existence as a martial order but soon became jovial indeed with much whoring, thieving, and corruption while keeping their holy robes. Dante is infuriated, for he recognizes these scoundrels and their infamy and is set to blast them with his righteous anger when his attention is pulled away by a figure lying prone beneath their feet.

Caiphus, the high priest of the temple, who piously gave Christ to the Romans, claiming it was better to give up one man in order that the nation be spared, lies crucified under the stomping feet of all the hypocrites. His hypocrisy is forced to bear the weight of every other.

Virgil finds not only their way out of the chasm but also learns that Malacoda, the little devil, has fibbed about his exit. Oh, those demons, you just can't trust 'em!

LIGHTEN UP WILL YA — HOW'D I KNOW HE REALLY WAS THE MESSIAH?

IS THERE ANY WONDER I GOT OPHIDIA PHOBIA!

Canto XXIV

Up they climb from the pit of hypocrisy. All the while, Dante muses on Virgil's relationship as shepherd to his poor little sheep. This poor little sheep is tuckered and stops to catch his breath, but the man with the staff admonishes, saying that he who stops for a snooze will evaporate like smoke. Fame goes to he whose soul pushes on!

Okay, I'm movin' already.

They reach the arch across the seventh *bolgia* and look down. This is the pouch of **thieves** who slid like snakes in life and now must suffer damnation with their scaly mentors. The reptiles coil about wrists, legs, find passage between thighs, binding all those who prospered by pilfering the wealth of others. One hapless criminal breaks free of the throng only to have a venomous spear leap out and find a soft target in his neck.

Upon the poison's injection, the bandit bursts into flame. Consumed to ashes, he falls. Miracles! The ashes form, reconstitute his being. He rises to suffer pain again.

He of the transformation is none other than **Vanni Fucci** whom Dante had known in his days of "blood and anger". He was sentenced to the snake pit for robbing a church sacristy and letting another man do the time. But chastened? Not he, for being recognized he makes dire predictions of the fates of Florence and Dante. Misery certainly does love company.

Canto XXV

Fucci, a man who could have taken residence in several different circles, is not finished until he raises both hands in "figs", an obscene gesture referring to the vulva, and shouts: "God, take these square in your face!"

A snake wraps about his throat to stop further blasphemy and Fucci, stoked by the fires of internal rage, races off just before **Cacus**, a stealing Centaur who had the misfortune of joining Hercules' club, comes looking for his surly carcass. Cacus isn't exactly a guard here.

His big horse haunches are swinging a grass skirt of stinging vipers and a fire-breathing dragon peeks over his shoulder to shout hello at everyone the old horse's ass meets. Cacus trots off the ever-shifting stage and is replaced by one of the inferno's most nightmarish retributions.

The five "noble" thieves of Florence rush into view, although only three are at the moment discernible. The others soon make their appearance known: **Agnello** is clutched in the obscene embrace and kiss of **Cianfa**, a six-legged serpent. Slowly as breath exchanges, Agnello grows more reptile, Cianfa more human, until the transformation is complete. **Buoso** is sucked at the navel by **Guercio**, who is but a small black lizard. Smoke flows from wound to mouth. As the tail of Guercio splits into legs, Buoso's join. Ears, arms, members grow, reside. The smoke clears, Guercio scampers to find a navel to suck, Buoso to avoid another slithery encounter. Only **Puccio** remains unchanged, but knows his shape will be stolen and he in turn will steal another, on and on and always the painful confusion of who is who, or are we both or neither?

Canto XXVI

Seeing the five Florentines, all of noble birth, so debased in the seventh *bolgia*. Dante laments the debasement of his own dear city. Such a place of nobility and glory turned to the lowest, thieving pursuits. It's too much, and Dante forces himself to break off as the eighth gulf beckons.

Dante is first reminded of the fireflies dancing their turn of light and darkness on the summer Tuscan hillsides, but these are not joyous mating bugs. These are the evil counselors, those who swayed with burning tongues now consigned to tongues of flame, each conscience to forever flicker in the dark of Hell.

IF ONLY I COULDA GOTTEN INTO TELEVISION.

Virgil calls one flame forth. It twins the souls of brave **Ulysses** and his friend **Diomedes**, both heroes and tricksters in the wars of Troy. Ulysses speaks of his last voyage. He has seen too much to sit content by Penelope's fire. He thirsts to know! He exhorts companions to join him in the greatest journey ever attempted, a cruise to follow the track of the sun, out beyond the Pillars of Hercules into the Western Sea. They sail past all human habitation and as they near the "other" pole (imagine the Earth with an east-west axis, instead of the north-south, with Jerusalem marking due east) they see a huge mountain stepping its way to heaven. This is **Mount Purgatory**, but no one can enter this way. A tempest arises. All hands are lost.

Canto XXVII

Ulysses, at Virgil's command, departs, and is replaced by yet another, one quivering and jumping with anticipation at hearing Italian spoken. It is **Guido de Montefeltro**, the "fox" of Romagna, and he begs word of his native land's affairs (remember, everyone can see the future but becomes blind at its transformation into the present). Dante relates a beautiful, albeit tabloid, version of current events and old Guido responds with his sad and surprising tale.

In Romagna, he railed against the Pope and rallied all to the Ghibelline cause, but he got old, "lost the wind in his sails" and decided to get himself to a monastery. There in Franciscan brown he's visited by none other than Pope Boniface VIII, old evil Peter himself. Dante thinks Boniface should be out rousing the troops to take back the Holy Land, but instead Boniface is engaged in securing his kingdom in this world and not the next, and had enlisted Guido's aid with the promise of "You breaka the rules, I giva da absolution," an offer Guido can't refuse. Imagine the shock when the **Black Cherubim**, the baddest of the bad angels, comes to snatch him by the short and curlies and gets into a tug of war with good St. Francis. The Black Cherubim, while claiming one doesn't need to be a logician to figure it out, explains:

"One who does not repent cannot be absolved and it is impossible to repent and cause a thing at the same time..."

Poor Guido trades the robes of heaven for a suit of flame. Ouch!

AIN'T NO SUCH THING AS A SURE THING.

Hey, you'll grow into it.

Canto XXXVIII

On the poets move to the ninth chasm: the **Sowers of Discord**. As these folks brought schism to their various endeavors so are they rendered asunder. They encounter **Mahomet**, known to us as Mohammed. An avenging demon armed with a sword does the surgery on all who must pass his way and in Mahomet's case, he is rent from chin to arsehole (Dante describes it as "the mouth that farts"). In Dante's time, Mahomet and his religion were considered as a heresy that split true Christian struggle in the East, and not a separate faith, hence the severance of East and West within his own body.

Mahomet is followed by his nephew **Ali**, who weeps uncontrollably for the blow that has parted his face from forelock to chin. Mahomet, however, does not weep, but warns that **Brother Dolcino**, a Franciscan who preached that the Church should go back to its simple apostolic origins and was thought by many to be a Communist and libertine, would join this hacked and hatcheted parade. He ended as shish-kabob with his mistress in 1307.

The troublemakers pass, each with an appropriate wound: maimed mouth for the vicious **gossip**, handless arms for the troublesome **rebel**, on and on. As they make their way around the ring, their hurts heal only to be opened again by the devil's blade. Some pains are completely beyond reason and Dante, this chronicler of all things impossible, hesitates to recount the injury of **Bertran de Born**, the great Provençal troubadour and unwise advisor to England's **Prince Henry**, convincing him to seize the throne from his own papa, Henry II. Bertran, for his sins has lost his head, carrying it before him like a lantern. He raises it to better converse with the poets who stand on the span across the canyon. So goes the punishment for he who would bring down the head of the family.

WELL, AT LEAST IT AIN'T STUCK UP MY . . .

YOU CUTTIN' IN LINE?

Canto XXIX

Dante lingers, feeling a terrible pain for our poor old world and its constant circle of strife, and wants a good cleansing cry. He also scans the mutilated crowd for his father's contentious cousin, **Geri del Bello**, who was not only a perpetrator, but a victim of Florence's internecine violence. Dante, ever the real human and never the righteous psalm singer, actually feels a vague and unreasonable guilt at never avenging his relative. Virgil exhorts Dante to keep moving, as it is already the morning of Holy Saturday and there is still much to see. Geri has indeed made his presence known with threatening gestures before being reabsorbed in the suffering legion.

Now they enter the tenth and last ditch of the Malebolge. This is the infernal realm of the **Falsifiers**, and their punishments are many. With four different classes, it's hard to keep track. The first class we encounter are the **Alchemists**, not the guys who were honestly engaged in scientific research, but they who falsified the things of nature. The smell of rot and decay is warning of their numerous afflictions. They of false concoctions suffer the vagaries of real disease. Two such sit back to back, their claws digging into their scabbed skins, their "scurf falling like fish scales". Another, **Cappocchio**, in the midst of his endless itching, addresses Dante as if he knows him, and surely the poet will attest to what a "good ape of nature" was he. Dante declines to testify.

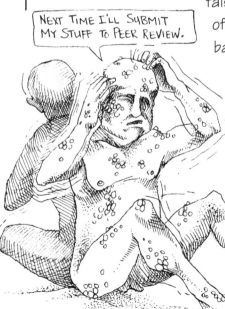

NEXT TIME I'LL SUBMIT MY STUFF TO PEER REVIEW.

Canto XXX

No matter Dante's silence, soon Cappochio's speech is stilled as another sinner, ravening like a rabid beast, sinks his teeth into the alchemist's throat and drags him off. This is **Gianni Schicchi**, a falsifier of persons, made famous by **Boccacio** and later honored with a short opera by **Puccini**. Gianni portrayed, at the bereaved family's insistence, a recently dead old gentlemen in order to favorably change a will. He is accompanied by **Myrrha**, she of ancient legend who so lusted for illicit congress with her father that she masqueraded as another to do the dirty deed. These false persons no longer can distinguish what they are: beast, man, woman?

Next we come to **Master Adam**, an ace **counterfeiter** of coin. He is not only afflicted with bloat, pus, and scale, but with unquenchable thirst—just try to buy a drink! He identifies a **forge**r, falsifier of word, as **Sinon of Troy**, the boy who didn't write his forgery but spoke it, convincing the besieged Trojans that a big wooden horse would look real keen in the town square. Sinon, crippled with the bloated limbs of dropsy, is unimpressed with Adam's collegial honesty and is just able to thud one heavy fist on his head. This sets off a nasty bout of the infernal dozens, adding insult to injury. Dante is much too entertained and Virgil rebukes his avid interest, saying,

> **"This place is filled with such battle—The desire to hear them is a degradation."**

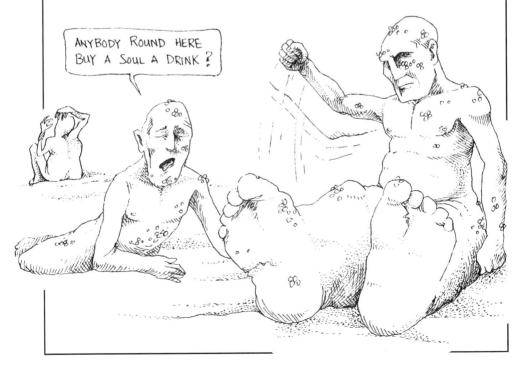

ANYBODY ROUND HERE BUY A SOUL A DRINK?

Canto XXXI

Virgil giveth and forgiveth, taking Dante sweetly through the gloom away from the Malebolge to some new fright. A horn blast pierces the fog. A huge figure and then others stand like towers in the fog. Here is the well of giants and at its bottom lies the deepest pit of Hell. He of the horn is **Nimrod**, the biblical builder, and he babbles: "Rafel Mai Amek Zabi Ami". For cursing the world with miscommunication when God struck his tower down, Nimrod prattles away in gibberish that not even he can understand. Others in the pit are **Ephialtes** who, with his brother, stormed the gates of heaven in one great jealous rage against the sky and **Tityos** who tried to kidnap **Apollo**'s mom. They are joined by **Antaeus**, another mama's boy, who had the misfortune of wrasslin' with Hercules and, while he couldn't be defeated with his tootsies in the dirt, was not such a great swimmer when Herc tossed him into the drink.

One might wonder at these Big Boys doin'
hard time in chains in this place. After all, an
attack on old Zeus might not be such an anti-
Christian thing. Antaeus was just an oversized
bully, but hey, what's a world to do with such
arrogant, lumbering troublemakers? If they
can't control themselves, they just gots ta be
controlled somehow!

Virgil convinces Antaeus that they simply
must use his hand as an elevator, and
sensing Dante's fear at such
a crushing possibility,

I HOPE YOU
PACKED A
SWEATER.

takes the poet lovingly
in his protective arms.
Down, down, down they
go. Down to "that ice
that swallows Lucifer
with Judas".

Canto XXXII

They leave the warm palm of Antaeus for the frozen center of the universe, the furthest place from God's light and love. This is **Cocytus**. All the rivers of the inferno spill here and freeze. It is divided into four concentric rings, each holding its quantity of traitors in order of offense. **Caina** is named for Cain, and contains those who betrayed kin. **Antenora** is named for Antenor who turned against his own country of Troy. **Ptolomaea**, called for Ptolomaeus, from the Old Testament Maccabees who murdered his father-in-law at a banquet, and last, the **Judecca**, which takes its title from Judas, and represents the place of damnation for those who turn on their benefactors. With each circle, the traitors lie buried deeper in the ice. Those of the Caina are allowed both head and neck freedom, and can at least turn downward from the ever blowing gale. This ice encases **Mordred**, the bastard son of **King Arthur**, who would not wait for succession and drove a spear through his sire at the Round Table's last battle.

I GUESS IT REALLY DOES FREEZE OVER!

As the poets continue into the Antenora, Dante accidentally kicks the head of one inmate, frozen to the chin. The iceman cries in pain and asks why he is being punished even further for Montaperti. Dante stops, intrigued. He certainly knows of the **Battle of Montaperti** and Florence's treacherous near defeat. Virgil quizzes the miscreant until Dante can no longer contain himself. He seizes the sinner's hair and, by his account, pulls hanks from the head. His intense anger brings forth the name **Bocca degli Abati**, a kinsman of Dante's own mother and his native land's foulest traitor. He is the one who took his sharp sword and lopped off the standard bearer's hand and only proud Farinata (he who resides just within the walls of Dis in a furnace of a heretics tomb) could turn the day. The yet living kinsman leaves off with disgust wishing no more commerce with this one.

Past **Ganelon**, the traitor of France's beloved **Roland**, they step by many more until they spy two heads so close in the ice one seems, "a cap for the other". Upon closer examination, this "cap" is gnawing through the skull of its close companion. Dante must know about this grim cannibalism and pledges, in return for the tale, to remember them in the world above.

I'D BE PULLIN' HAIR IF THAT ILLUSTRATOR HAD DRAWN YOU ANY!

Canto XXXIII

The eater is **Count Ugolino** and his meal, **Archbishop Ruggieri**. Ugolino was a powerful Ghibelline of Pisa who, in the interests of more power, turned Guelph and conspired against his former cohorts. Eventually he allied himself with the Archbishop and together they consolidated all of Pisa in their grubby mitts, even bargaining away various hill forts and castles to other cities to achieve their aims. But Ruggieri proved himself the greater traitor by seizing Ugolino and his four young sons and sealing them in a tower. Thus begins Hell's most affecting tale, which along with Paolo and Francesa and Ulysses' last adventure stirs our sympathy.

Days pass. The inmates' only calendar is watching the change of moon and sun through the window. No food or drink is offered. Hunger gnaws at empty bellies. The sons offer their father a poignant and impossible meal:

> **"Father... you did clothe us in this sorry flesh;
> it is for you to strip it off again."**

The father tries to calm his sons. His oldest begs: "Father, why don't you help me?" By the sixth day, Ugolino, blinded by famine, crawls from son to son and finds each finally calmed by death.

Ugolino finishes his sad recitation with the enigmatic statement: "Then fasting overcame my grief". Did Ugolino eat earth's most sinful meal following his son's instruction? Did death come to stop the torture of his loss in this world if certainly not the next? It is probably the latter, but Ugolino has no cannibalistic qualms in the Antenora as he sets to his eternal meal again.

The poets step forward into the wind. Dante inquires as to its origin. Virgil gives him a "You'll see" as they come to the Ptolomea. Here the **traitors to hospitality** lie frozen with only their faces revealed. Their tears weld crying eyes tight without the prospect of ever opening. Here also lie the only truly living denizens of the inferno. These traitors, without any shred of repentance, send their souls below while their bodies still move about on the earth above. So it is with **Brother (Fra) Alberigo** and **Branca D'Oria**. Brother Alberigo, a Jovial Friar, had been slighted by his brothers. Pretending there was no problem, he invited them to a banquet. Fruit was offered, its sweetness bittered with poison. Alberigo states, "Here I get dates for my figs," meaning his little game lands

him a morsel of more value, a just dessert.

Branca D'Oria is also a bad meal ticket. He sent invitations to his pop-in-law, **Michel Zanche** (no saint himself, he was dispatched to *bolgia* five with the barrators), and had him and his cronies minced as part of the festivities. The soul is lost forever but the body can still play host at other feasts. Chew on that.

Canto XXXIV

The **Judecca**—the deepest abyss, the last circle of Hell.
No heads are visible here. All bodies lie contorted under
the ice. These, the **sinners against those who only
wished them well**, are obliterated, the traitors who
are so completely immersed in their crime that no
other display of humanity is possible.

"Onward march the banners of the King of
Hell," Virgil parodies a hymn popular during Holy
Week and at last, Dante sees the cause of the
arctic blast. **Lucifer** (Dis), he who sat at God's feet,
the former Lord of Light, stands frozen in the ice at
the very heart of Hell. His once beautiful visage is
made ugly by his incredible crime. Where angel's
wings had once sprouted now stretch giant bat-like
appendages beating furiously to free the giant form,
but ironically, the harder they flap, the colder the
wind, and the stronger the impossibility of hell
ever thawing.

91

Lucifer's head is disfigured in a grotesque parody of the Blessed Trinity. An angry red face resides in front, a sickly white and yellow to the right side and a black face to the left. Six eyes weep tears of blood and pus. Three mouths chew in pain and impotent rage three, the worst, sinners. **Judas Iscariot**, the Betrayer of Christ, kicking and screaming, fills the center maw, and at times, his whole back is flayed and ripped away.

Brutus is the black mouth's meal and **Cassius** the white's. To us it may seem strange to have these two almost co-equal with he who propelled the sacrifice of Christ, but the assassination of **Julius Caesar** and the attempt to thwart the establishment of the Roman Empire was, to Dante, an unbelievable action, tantamount to supplanting God's natural rule on earth.

Virgil approaches the great fiend. Dante huddles behind the Roman poet's gale-breaking form. As they make the hairy side, Virgil commands Dante to clasp him around the neck, and with an opening available between the pounding wings, he rushes in and seizes the devil's shag and climbs downward a cleft in the ice.

Down they climb. At one point sensing the shift in gravity (yes, Dante had a sense of the earth's attraction, but was certainly no Newton), Virgil turns the other direction where down becomes up. Virgil explains that when Lucifer fell, he was driven feet first into the earth. He caused the huge crater of the inferno on the topside and pushed the displaced soil into the Mount of Purgatory on the other. They make their progress to that mountain of salvation.

At last, on Easter morning, the travelers reach the open air. Above them wink the stars of heaven.

The Purgatorio

Canto I

The sun's light begins to color the east. The light of four stars, the four cardinal virtues—**prudence, justice, fortitude** and **temperance**—almost equal the sun's rising rays, and bathe Virgil's face in a holy light. Dante calls on **Calliope**, the Muse of epic poetry, to help him describe the soul's adventure to follow. But such reverie is soon disturbed by the stern arrival of **Cato of Utica**.

Cato, although a pagan and a suicide, was given special status in the Middle Ages. His death was considered martyrdom to a higher cause, the founding of a just state. Now he haunts the slope leading to the Mount of Purgatory. And haunt he does with a vengeance. The old man suspects he's caught a couple of escapees from Hell and only Virgil's explanations can keep them from returning to the fire and ice.

Cato relents not for the invocation of his late wife, Marcia; he seems beyond her now. He relents because **Beatrice**, that "heavenly dame", has commanded Virgil to assume this journey with poor awestruck Dante. But before entry is allowed a little preparation must be done.

Down to the shore of the southern ocean the poets go. And on that gentle bank, Virgil, following Cato's orders, gathers dew from the wet grass. Softly he cleanses Dante's face of Hell grime and bathes his tired eyes. Next, he plucks a reed to wrap the Florentine's waist, a sign of humility, and oh marvel! Another grows instantly in its place. Renewal is here.

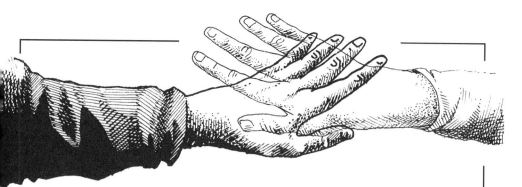

Canto II

After his brief but claustrophobic and frightening sojourn in Hell, Dante can't fill his eyes and heart with enough of the sights of this new world, a world so wondrously close to Heaven. As he gazes across the sea, he spies a light, white unlike the sun, scudding quickly across the waves to this very shore. It is an angelic barge filled with souls ready to begin their ascent to the skies above. They disembark and, still disorientated with this new place, seek directions from Virgil. But hey, this place is just as new to him. The souls are shocked as they turn to Dante. He breathes! Dante explains, and as he does, he catches sight of his dear friend, **Casella**. He tries to give him a hug, but no go. His arms pass right through. These shades cast none. The inferno still clings to the corporeal. In this place flesh is cast from spirit.

Casella, who has been delayed entry for a few months, explains how all of these souls who did the jubilee were gathered at the mouth of the river Tiber for a quick trip to the Netherworld. Dante, ever the curious, asks Casella if his singing voice has been affected by his recent demise. Casella responds with a song of Dante's composition: "Love speaks reason to my mind…"

"What's going on?" Cato rushes up, speeding these dawdlers like doves up the hillside. Time is wastin'.

Canto III

Virgil is a bit upset. He really shouldn't have tarried to listen to a little music. Dante sees his loving master upset at such a small thing, and is suddenly startled to see, with the sun at their backs, only one shadow. Hey, told you these "shades" cast none, but Dante didn't hear, so Virgil must explain this strange phenomenon of the Afterlife. One is but isn't. Reason cannot answer everything. Sometimes a person just has to accept the "Quiva" (fact) of the thing. If reason could explain the whole schmear, there wouldn't be a "reason" for a religion, would there?

ME AND MY SHADOW?

As they converse, they notice a new "flock" of souls (sheep, doves, these purgatorial folks conjure up nice pastoral images for our poet) making their way up from shore to mountain. Virgil must ask directions up—this ain't his usual stompin' ground. They discover something of the nature of this spiritual place and how it operates. Time for a map:

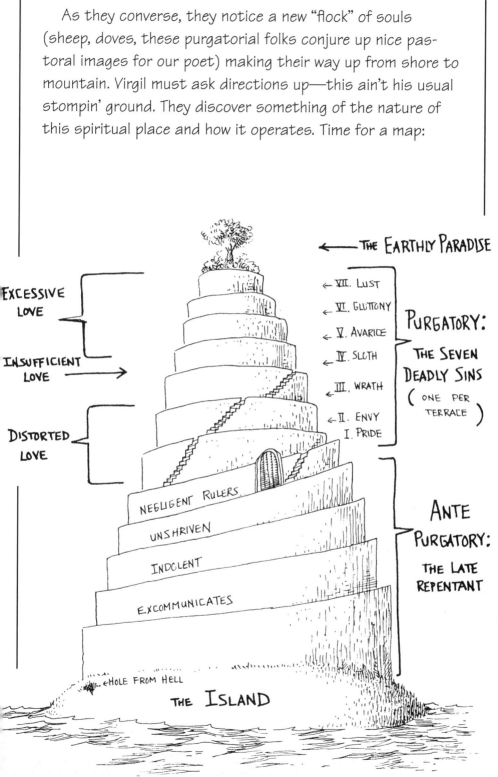

THE EARTHLY PARADISE

EXCESSIVE LOVE

INSUFFICIENT LOVE

DISTORTED LOVE

← VII. LUST
← VI. GLUTTONY
← V. AVARICE
← IV. SLOTH
← III. WRATH
← II. ENVY
I. PRIDE

PURGATORY:
THE SEVEN DEADLY SINS
(ONE PER TERRACE)

NEGLIGENT RULERS
UNSHRIVEN
INDOLENT
EXCOMMUNICATES

ANTE PURGATORY:
THE LATE REPENTANT

←HOLE FROM HELL
THE ISLAND

The new group is made up of sinners who delayed repentance until the last moment and are set out for Ante-Purgatory, a place of waiting until they can gain access to one of the terraces of Purgatory proper. One quick way of gaining entry is via the prayers of the living, and every sinner in this vast waiting area will ask Dante to convey their requests to those loved ones still among the quick. This becomes a spiritual burden for Dante, one he welcomes. He is first thus encumbered by **Manfred**, the grandson of the Emperor **Henry VI** and **Constance**, and son of **Frederick II**, who was a Ghibelline darling and anti-papal claimant of the throne defeated at Benevento in 1266. His body was buried in consecrated ground, but Pope Clement said "no way, that boy was excommunicated and his body goes to the river bank". Well, his body may have been given the boot, but there is a higher claim on his soul! Thus Manfred has joined the troop of fellow excommunicates on this spiral up the mountain. He only asks Dante to have his daughter Constance "say a little prayer for me".

WELL, KID, IT'S ALL UPHILL FROM HERE.

Canto IV

Dante has spent so much time in conversation, the morning is almost shot—he gives rise to the thinking person's "can't walk and chew thoughts at the same time". Virgil exhorts him onward and upward in the excommunicates' direction to the next spiral of Ante-Purgatory. Dante is pretty puffed out by the climb. Virgil assures him it gets progressively easier as they scale closer and closer to Heaven and eventually reach the earthly Paradise, a place beyond reason.

Whew! Tiring stuff, but then this is the home of the indolent, and lo and behold, here lies Dante's pal, **Belacqua**. Belacqua was famous for his procrastination. A prayer from the Northern Hemisphere would put dynamite under his butt. Hint, hint.

Well, I meant to give at the office.

Canto V

There is, of course, a lighter and hopeful tone suffusing the entirety of the *Purgatorio*, but still Dante knows when to bring the pathos in to play. Making their way to the next level, they encounter a new group of souls who are fascinated with this visitor from the "first" life. Virgil urges Dante to not let chitchat slow them, but nonetheless, there are some moving stories here.

All of these folks met violent ends, and due to the quickness of their deaths were unable to receive the last rites. **Buonconte da Montefeltro** was one of Dante's comrades-in-arms at the Battle of Campaldino. He lies unshriven in an unknown grave, for he fled the field mortally wounded with a second mouth beneath his chin, one that leaked his blood and allowed his upper mouth one brief parting word: "Mary". Taken up by an angel, he cheated Hell by that one utterance.

Pia, the only name we learn, tells her poignant tale in so few lines:

> "Sienna birthed me; Maremma, death.
> And he whom I wed
> Taking his circled gem, is he who made me dead."

Canto VI

The other souls crowd in, hoping for remembrance in the prayers of the living. When they are free of the press of the unshriven, Dante asks how it can be that God is swayed to action by the thoughts spoken at him from a loved one. Virgil explains that God is not moved by such entreaties. There is a subtler action involved, an action that he does not understand but that will, in short order, be reasoned at the top of the mountain by Beatrice. Yowsa! Let's move it on up!

As they hustle, the shade of **Sordello**, a poet who wrote beautiful verse in Provençal and as a favorite of Charles of Anjou became involved in enough intrigue to land him in Ante-Purgatory, springs forth to bear-hug his fellow Mantuan, Virgil. This show of civil affection plunges Dante into a reverie at once seeing the joys of imperial fraternity and despairing the existing conditions of severance and strife in Italy and the world.

Canto VII

When Sordello fully realizes that this Mantuan is none other than Virgil, he falls to his knees, 'cause Virgil is the man. Sordello explains that once he's back on his feet, the rules of Purgatory are such that no upward progress can take place in darkness, only in the full light of God's brightly shining face. He will lead them on to the **Valley of the Kings** for the night and then, in the morning, on to **St. Peter's Gate**, the demarcator of Purgatory from Ante-Purgatory.

The valley, chiseled into the side of the mountain, is a pretty spectacular place. It is a place of natural luxury. Soft grass, bright and fragrant blossoms, and shapely trees. Virgil notes that it is much like his digs in limbo with one huge exception: nobody abandons hope here. They live hope, for they are on their way out to more abundant climes. The place is populated by negligent rulers who let statecraft get in the way of repentance. Dante notes many of the folks connected with the Holy Roman Empire, **Rudolf I**, chief amongst 'em, and one lone **Henry II**, father of Richard the Lionheart, **Prince John** (hiss, boo) and Hank, Jr of England, who took Bertran De Born's advice. Lest one imagine that it's easier to get to Heaven with a crown on your brow, Dante is

very careful to in-
sist that it is
the person and
not the circum-
stances of
birth that
puts one in
the cosmic
hierarchy.

Canto VIII

At last, the sun sinks. Three stars twinkle above the South Pole representative of the three theological virtues: faith, hope, and charity. The voices of the rulers are raised in the hymn of the end of day. All seems peaceful, but not exactly. Sordello notifies the visiting poets that they ain't quite in Purgatory yet, and they're still subject to temptation. This pretty garden would be a likely place for a snake visit. As if on cue, two leaf-green angels with flaming swords, broken short of the points, come straight from Mary's bosom to clear the path of reptiles. Yikes, snakes! Poor Dante snuggles up close to Virgil as Sordello takes them into the valley.

They encounter **Nino**, Judge of Gallura, an old friend of Dante's and he in turn summons **Conrad Malaspina**. As they talk in the soft twilight, Dante praises the house of Malaspina (one of the hospitable families during his exile), until they are interrupted by the green angels doing some vermin control. Old snake slinks off, having come within striking distance of the Judge.

Canto IX

Dante discovers just how lush and giving the lawn of this valley is, and promptly curls up into a deep sleep. Remember, he hasn't had a wink since before he got lost in the woods. He dreams of a great golden eagle circling in the air above him. It stoops and grasps Dante in its talons. Together they ascend, up into the realm of fire.

They are consumed in a conflagration of ecstasy.

Whoa! Dante starts awake to find that it is morning, and he and Virgil are standing before the Gates of St. Peter. Seems Dante's dream was more real than fantasy and **St. Lucia** (Lucia = Light, she's taken over Lucifer's job) has transported them to this spot.

An angel with a whole sword aflame sits magnificently on a stoop rising from three steps. These steps represent the Catholic sacrament of penance: the first white step reflects the sinner in the full knowledge of **contrition**, the second purple-black riser is the sorrow of **confession**, and the last blood-red step is the true love that opens the way for **absolution**. Virgil responds to the angel's inquiry of identification, and they move forward to the golden gate cut in the rampart blocking Purgatory from it's ante.

THANK GOODNESS I MINDED MY "Q"s.

PPPPPPP

The angel deftly marks Dante's brow with seven P's They are the "peccatas", sins, that delineate the mountain's seven terraces. They can only be washed within. The angel reaches into his ash colored vestment and pulls forth two keys, gold and silver, on loan from Peter, the only picks for opening this lock and with a roar of hinges and a chorus of "te deum laudamus" (we praise thee, o God), the poets enter Purgatory.

Canto X

The gate opens into a narrow and torturously winding passage that Dante dubs the "eye of the needle" as in a difficult place for a rich man to squeeze through. The poets, after hours of wedging and heaving to do just that, step into the open shelf of the **prideful**. Carved into the white marble wall of the mount are three incredible instances of **humility**, that antidote to pride.

The first *bas relief* is of **Mary** on the glorious morning when **Gabriel** swooped out of Heaven to inform her of her miraculous "big event" to come. The second panel depicts **David**, the psalmist, less and more of a king dancing before the Ark of the Covenant. The last panel is a story from pagan history, so moving that Pope and Saint **Gregory** prayed that the emperor involved be brought back to life and baptized so he could enter Heaven. It shows the emperor **Trajan** being accosted as he rode forth with his legions, by a poor woman who only sought justice for her murdered son. Touched with compassion, the Roman Caesar halted his armies to instead take up the grieving mother's cause.

Dante's attention is startled by a movement of huge boulders along the ledge toward them. He can barely believe that beneath each burden is a soul of one atoning for their earthly pride. Each groan seems a plea: "no more".

Canto XI

As the prideful creep closer, Dante discerns that their moans are actually a version of the Paternoster, the Lord's Prayer, redesigned for this location. It's main difference is its most fervent request for easing the troubles of those souls left behind in

IT AIN'T HEAVY IT'S MY SIN.

the first life, for these praying souls, even with their terrible weights are definitely on the road to Heaven. **Omberto of Sienna**, a man overly proud of his noble birth, leads the way. Dante recognizes **Oderisi of Gubbio**, a famous illuminator of manuscripts. Oderisi at last can admit that his pupil and rival, **Franco of Bologna**, is the better painter. This humble truth sets Dante on a mini-discourse about the swiftly turning nature of the arts. In the painting of frescoes, **Cimabue** will be supplanted by **Giotto**. And in poetry, the great versifier, **Guido Guinizelli** will be replaced by old Dante himself. But, oh, sobering thought, Dante will be replaced by he who will follow. You can't stop time.

They spy **Provenzan Salvani**, an arrogant Sienese, who bent the entire city to his will. He put off repentance but landed here because of one famous act of humility. A friend was imprisoned by **King Charles** who put a high ransom on his skin. Salvani stepped into Sienna's marketplace and begged alms until he had enough to spring his pal. Hey, that's what friends are for!

Canto XII

Once again Virgil urges Dante to haste and the poet consents, but with a new humility. As they step, Virgil instructs
Dante's vision to the ground on which they walk. It is carved
with thirteen tableaux of pride brought low: **Lucifer, Nimrod,
Holofernes, Troy.** From Olympus to doormat so falls pride.
Dante plays a little literary game with the description of
these panels. The first four begin with "Vedea," (I saw), the V
equivalent to our U The next with O, the last with
"Mostravia" (it showed) and then back to "Vedea," Put it together and the letters spell "Uomo"—man. Man equals pride!

The poets come to a white robed angel whose face "trembles like at star at morn". The angel graciously leads them to
a stairway up to the next tier, it's wing brushing Dante's brow.
As they ascend the stairs, Virgil notices one P has been
erased by a wing and the other six made shallower—once
pride is defeated, all other sins become easier to face and
conquer. The angel sweetly sings, "Beati Pauperes Spiritu,"
blessed are the poor in spirit, as they easily step upward.

GEE, I THINK
I'LL TAKE A
SMALLER HATSIZE
NOW.

Canto XIII

As the poets mount the stairs let us digress a moment. Please notice that the map (page 97) delineates the seven tiers of Purgatory into three separate zones: distorted love, insufficient love and excessive love. As is apparent, Dante was the poet of love. **Love** is the operating force of the universe. Love is God. God is love. Hell is love denied. So, Purgatory represents perversion of love, but, thank goodness, perversion is still some kind of love. To crawl up the mountain is to have a love adjustment. Once everything is fixed you have nowhere to go but up! Speaking of up, the poets step out on the next terrace. It is cut from dark stone and its expanse appears empty. Virgil prays:

> "O blessed light, in you we place our trust
> as we make our way in this new place..."

"Vinum non habent," "They have no wine," a disembodied voice cries echoing Mary's words to Jesus at the marriage feast in Cana. "I am Orestes" cries another voice, repeating the loving phrase of **Pylades** who sought to prevent his friend's execution. It is evident that this is the tier of the **envious** and the ringing declamations are examples of pure, unjealous, generous love.

Soon Virgil and Dante spy the souls gathered in a hollow in the cliff. They lean together, offering each other the support they refused in life, dressed in hairshirts, eyelids sewn together with wire. As they disliked the good they saw, now they see nothing.

Dante speaks with them. A Sienese woman named **Sapia** responds with her story. She was a resident of Latium and terribly envious of her birthplace, Sienna. When Sienna was defeated by Florence at the Battle of Colle, she rejoiced. Now with her new sympathy she actually notices others. In fact, isn't Dante, her interrogator, breathing?

Dante explains his mission and in a display of naked honesty predicts that he will not spend much time in the next life with his eyes closed. There's a big rock reserved for him on the tier below.

Canto XIV

Dante gets into a discussion with two more spirits, **Guido del Duca** and **Rinieri da Calboli.** This discussion is the now familiar one decrying the inhabitants of cities along the Arno, i.e. Florence, and the deplorable conditions in northern Italy in general. Dante, along with his growing virtue, still has a bone to pick. This bone leaves his ghostly commentators in tears.

GOING UP?

As the poets move onward, another voice rips through the air, "Everyone that finds me shall slay me," the words of that poster boy for envy, **Cain**. And then, "I am Aglauros who was turned to stone." **Aglauros** was a sister of **Herse** and the god **Mercury**'s squeeze, and boy did she have the green eyes for old feather-feet. Mercury's annoyance with the situation only subsided when he turned Aglauros into a stone lawn ornament. This prompts Virgil into a metaphor's metaphor, complete with humans needing to keep God's bit in their mouths, but they just spit it out and get a bite of Hell's bait. All the while, God and his splendors wheel about above and man keeps his eyes peeled on the dirt. No wonder love has to smack us up the side of the head!

Canto XV

An angel, so bright as to hurt Dante's eyes, comes swooping to direct them to the stairs leading to the next level. They step, another P vanishes from Dante's brow, to the hymn, "Beati Misericordes," "Blessed are the merciful" (another of the Beatitudes, from the sermon on the mount that here signal the leave-taking of each sin) and then "Rejoice—you have overcome".

Dante asks Virgil for some clarification on the nature of envy. Virgil explains that envy is rooted in the need for material things, and the more one acquires, the less there is for others. It destroys true human partnership, whereas the more noble attributes one acquires, love, courage, knowledge, etc., the more there is for others. Envy fixes one on the transient material instead of the spiritual eternal.

As they step to the third level, the cornice of the **wrathful**, Dante has a vivid hallucination. He is buoyed by a crowd in the Temple of Jerusalem. **Jesus**, the lad, has been instructing the elders while neglecting the anxiety of his parents. Tenderly, the Virgin Mother instructs him, not with anger, but with an urge to compassion, "Your Father and I have sought you in sorrow".

Another vision replaces this: a different woman is weeping, begging her husband, **King Pisistratus**, to avenge their daughter who has been embraced by a too-eager youth. Pisistratus sagely asks, "what will we do to those who harm us if we take revenge on those who love us?"

A third, terrifying scene sweeps in. An angry mob, clutching at stones screams: "Kill! Kill!". The object of their wrath, gentle **Stephen**, is a convert to Christ's teachings. The stones do their work, raining on the boy's head even as he prays that God forgive them. This is a re-enactment of the Church's first martyrdom.

THERE HAS GOT TO BE AN EASIER WAY TO GET TO HEAVEN.

Mesmerized, Virgil urges Dante to continue on. The hour is late and soon they'll be forced

to stop.
As the sun
dips, the light is
further obscured by
a billowing cloud of
smoke.

Desire is like having alligators in the bathtub; they ain't a problem 'til you take 'em out and try to dry 'em off.

Canto XVI

The smoke grows thicker, acrid and stinging. Dante must clutch at Virgil's sleeve trusting the Mantuan to lead him through this foul murk. Voices singing the "Agnus Dei," the Lamb of God, urge pacification of this angry air.

Marco Lombardo pushes through the smoke to help lead them on the way. They fall into a discussion about the nature of evil in the world at the present time, obviously a subject to which Marco has given a great deal of thought. It all stems from free will, a thing neither good nor bad. The simple soul of a child comes into the world and is delighted by all God's creation. It follows one desire after another. Free will must be tempered with instruction, or the child will be tossed forever on this merry-go-round of desire. Instruction must come from above, and in things with earthly, temporal authority. But here's the problem: the church, by grasping after power and wealth in the world has set the worst possible example. If the Pope won't let Caesar do his job and get on with his own spiritual guidance, is it any wonder the first life is a place of tumult and turmoil?

Marco does suggest that one look at the sterling examples of **Currado da Palazzo**, the good **Gerard** and **Guido da Castel**, all noble and courageously honest councilors, as exemplars for the leadership sorely needed. At this point, light, an attribute of an arriving angel, pierces the fog and Marco, as one who must continue suffering the nasty, blinding conditions of his own anger, must depart, for he has yet to be granted the sight of this celestial creature.

Canto XVII

As the smoke breaks up, Dante is once again assaulted by visions, this time of unmitigated **anger**. **Procne** avenges her sister who was raped by her husband by serving their own son for dinner! **Haman**, because one Jew refused to bow, ordered all Jews killed. Instead, he was crucified. And **Amata**, a mother scorned by her daughter, hanged herself in her rage. Yowsa! Anger is like playing with matches and burning yourself. The lessons are learned in time for the angel's brush of wing, and another erasure of P and the revelation of the next staircase up. This time, the voice intones "Beati Pacifici," "Blessed are the peacemakers".

OH NO, THIS IS JUST LIKE WATCHING PRIME TIME TELEVISION.

Night is falling as they reach the fourth terrace, and it is impossible to continue. Virgil, to answer a question from Dante, explains that they are now on the tier of **sloth** where too-little-love is redeemed. Natural love, the love of a being for God, is completely without error. Rational love, the love we ourselves "think" up, can go astray. It can lead us in a perverse way against our neighbors as in pride, envy and wrath. It can be insufficient in the case of sloth or be too much like avarice, gluttony and lust. All of these loves get in the way of our perception and pursuit of natural love. We can only find out in what way we might be perverting rational love by searching inside ourselves, and ultimately surrendering the dissatisfactions of loves that will never fully quench our thirst for love divine.

Canto XVIII

Virgil continues to answer Dante's pressing questions on love and its implications. Love, and here one might substitute "desire", is a matter of attraction to a particular object. This attraction, when fulfilled, creates delight. This attraction, except in the case of natural love, is neither bad nor good. It may be either. If it conflicts with ethics, which are ordained by the honest pursuit of natural love, then it is bad. If it follows and enables us to come closer to the divinity, it is good. We are free to choose what course to pursue.

ALL YA NEED IS LOVE. LOVE IS ALL YA NEED. SI, SI, SI.

Virgil is not able
to explain more to his
pupil. Beatrice will have to
take up the chalk (or maybe
Thomas Aquinas, whose ideas
are central to this argument). In any
case, their discussion is interrupted
by the slothful, dancing, running,
shouting, energetic. Two of them pace
ahead announcing the zeal of the Virgin
and Caesar as examples to be followed.
The rest hop and skip behind with their pleas and prayers. The
cavalcade rushes on and blessed sleep arrives for Dante.

Canto XIX

Dante dreams. A squinty, hunched and altogether hideous
woman appears. The warmth of the sun drives cold and
crook from her limbs. She straightens. She blooms in
beauty. She sings. Ahhh. A "lady of heaven"
rushes in and exhorts Virgil to do his
duty. Virgil for his part rips the
concealing garments from
the siren. She is un-
clean. The stench
of filth rises
from her
belly.

sheep, no, sheep...

"Dante! Dante!" Virgil shakes the Florentine awake, "Three times I have called you". Dante stirs and shuffles along. The passage upward to the fifth terrace is revealed by the angel of zeal and with a wing's breath, Dante fills with new resolve as the souls intone the "Qui Lugent," "Blessed are they that mourn".

The fifth terrace is the palace of **avarice**, greed. The **hoarders** and their reflection, the **wasters**, lie in the dust, trussed like turkeys, wing and foot. They weep for the use of grasping hands. Dante seeks to engage one of the backsides in conversation. A voice responds, the voice of **Pope Adrian V**. He tells his tale of only coming to his senses once he was ordained Pope—it's about time! Dante falls to his knees next to the groveling Pontiff. Adrian instructs him to straighten his legs and get on with it. Oh, and the prayers of his niece, **Alagia**, ain't such a bad idea either.

You hear this one—a priest, a monk and a bishop walk into a bank . . .

Canto XX

They continue amongst the weeping prostrates. Dante wonders when greed, the old she-wolf, will depart the Earth. None too soon methinks. Some recall the stories of those who generously gave: the **Virgin Mary**, ancient **Fabricius** who remained virtuous against bribes, good **Saint Nicholas** (that's right, Santa Claus), and on.

One voice is that of **Hugh Capet**, King of France, and a hell of a land grabber: Ponthieu, Normandy and Gascony seized, and Provence made to pay tribute. Mister Avaricious on a grand scale. They continue to hear stories, but this time they learn of the greedy guts of history and myth. **Pilate** comes to mind and **Pygmalion**,— not the sculptor, but **Dido**'s bro who killed her husband for gold. The litany ends with **Crassus** who was so famously besotted with gold, his enemies fed his corpse the molten variety.

TH-TH-THERE'SSSS A WHOLE LOTTA-TA-TA SH-SH-SHAKIN GOIN' OOOOOOOOON**!!!**

As the voices hush, the mountain is seized with a violent and, as Dante will attest, frightening quake. From all around voices cry, "Gloria in excelsis deo," "Glory to God in the highest". Dante is left with a mixture of fear and wonder.

Canto XXI

The poets hurry along until their progress is halted by an approaching soul. The soul, after ascertaining that Virgil and Dante are on a special mission above, explains the earthquake. As once an inmate has willed to sin, they now will to suffer. When the will to suffer meets the equal desire to rise to glory, the soul rises, the mountain trembles, and another spirit goes to Paradise. A certain cause for Heaven and Earth to celebrate!

So who is this knowledgeable fellow? None other than the Latin poet, **Statius**, author of the *Thebiad* and the *Achilleid*. Statius, a truly humble soul, has one great hero and is not shy to praise him—Virgil, himself. Virgil sees Dante begin to smile but wants no word said. Oh well, alright, tell him. At this introduction, Statius falls to his knees. "Get up!" Virgil commands with embarrassment. It just isn't seemly for one spook to curtsey to another.

> I AM LIKE UNTO THE DUST UNDER VIRGIL'S FEET, of course, technically he became dust before I did, so — oh well, POETIC LICENSE.

POET! FORGET THAT— YOU'RE AN EVANGELIST AND DON'T KNOW IT!

Canto XXII

The poets three, having passed the sin-wiping angel, make their steps up to the sixth terrace. Virgil asks Statius how in creation he landed with the avaricious. Statius admits he wasn't greedy, he was wasteful, but mainly he was sloth-like. Seems he converted to Christianity due to the near prophecy contained in Virgil's own fourth *Ecologue*. The *Ecologue* speaks of a miraculous child born to a people of Iron—it sounds a lot like **Isaiah** in the Bible. Statius' interest was piqued, so he sought out the Christians. Voila! Conversion. Of course, he kept it on the quiet, as the Emperor **Domitian** was busy roasting his co-religionists like wienies. But 'tis better to have loved a little, than not at all (or actually better to have Dante writing your bio as all of Statius' is invented).

Statius has a few questions of his own: What happened to **Terrence** and **Plautus, Caccilius** and **Varro**? "They all be in Limbo with me," Virgil answers, "and everybody from **Euripides** to **Antigone**, as well." Hell of a place this Limbo, but still a place in Hell.

At last they get to the cornice of gluttony. A beautiful fruit tree breaks the horizon. A voice from out of the leaves informs of those who would go light on the feed for the greater glory: the Blessed Virgin Mary, the women of Rome who subsisted on water, **Daniel** who bypassed the food line for wisdom, and old crazy **John the Baptist** who had the taste for honey and locusts. Yum!

Canto XXIII

Dante slows to check those leaves for their speaking apparatus, much to his "more-than-father's" pleas to get the lead out. Another song sings out, "Labia me, domine," "Lord open thou my lips". The singers are the souls of the **gluttons** looking to the world like models on a fashion runway. So thin are they that all their faces spell the same word. The curve of brow meets the jutting ridge of nose giving an M surrounding eye O's, "omo," man. A sorrier bunch of men or women was never seen. Dante recognizes his friend, **Forese**.

Forese extols the sacred torture, the maddening perfume of ripe fruit urges on the moritification of the suffering flesh. He also extols the prayers of his beloved widow, **Nella**. Her ministrations have chipped more than a few years off his sentence. Would that all Florentine women showed such virtue. Instead, Forese rails, they have to be condemned from the pulpit for going about with breasts exposed to the "paps" (yet another fruit forbidden to taste).

Canto XXIV

As Forese gets his steamer really hissing, all the souls notice Dante's shadow. Dante, once again, goes into his old routine, "me and my shadow".

Forese lingers with his old friend. He points out various gluttons as they do their two-dimensional shuffle-by. One of the souls is **Bonagiunta da Lucca**, an old-school poet. He stops to ask Dante about the "sweet" new school of poetry. Dante simply states that it is love that inspires and dictates his words, to which Bonagiunta exclaims that, if only he and his brethren had allowed for such naturalism, they could have written as well. He leaves with a prophesy of a coming child of Lucca, named **Gentucca**, who will ease his bad feelings for her fellow citizens— which she did by helping Dante in his exile.

THE PROBLEM WITH FLORENCE TODAY IS THE PEOPLE IN IT! EXCUSE MY SUBTLETY.

As the reader might remember, Forese was not only our poet's buddy, but also the brother of his greatest enemy, Corso Donati. The brother sees his brother's death. Corso trying to gain the rule of Florence is arrested for his treachery. He slips and is dragged by his horse. All will transpire soon. At this, Dante departs and comes with his companions to the **tree of knowledge** (a chip off the old block, as it were, from the one in the garden).

More voices issue forth warning off they who know no temperance. **Eve** who knows none. The **Centaurs** who gorged and drunk at a wedding feast and tried to make off with the tastiest morsel, the bride. The old **Hebrews** whose thirst supplanted their etiquette and, against **Gideon**'s God-ordained command, lapped from the stream like dogs.

At this the angel of **abstinence**, a glowing-red of such intensity that Dante is temporarily blinded, brushes yet another P from the poet's forehead. Amidst the ambrosial fragrance, voices declaim a paraphrase of a beatitude: "Blessed are they who are so illuminated by grace that they hunger not for taste, but rather for the just measure".

I THOUGHT YOU'D GO BLIND IF YOU DIDN'T ABSTAIN.

Canto XXV

As they make their way to the next
level, Dante is in a bit of a quandary. Virgil,
ever gracious and aware of his pagan status,
defers to Statius for enlightenment. Dante
simply wants to know why, in the absence of
physical bodies are the gluttons skinny?

The answer entails a great deal of scholastic
philosophy and mistaken biology (remember, we are talkin'
early fourteenth century here). The scholastics were the
church thinkers influenced primarily by Aristotle. **St. Thomas
Aquinas** (1227-74) was chief among them. Most of Dante's
thought is an interpretation of Aquinas (who we'll meet in
the Paradiso).

Here goes (with a sexist alert!): there exists a "perfect
blood" that doesn't actually flow through the veins but
rather resides in the heart. In the heart of a father it transforms into sperm. With procreation the sperm acts on the
passive blood of the female to form the fetus. The fetus,
most definitely possessed of a soul, goes through all the
stages of life: the vegetative, the animal and the human.
What separates the human soul from the others is the
"breath" of God, which fills every human with an intellect
(here we are informed of the medieval Aristotelian, **Averroes'**
mistaken belief that there was no differentiation in soul, the
human's being simply hooking into a universal "possible intellect"). When the body dies, the soul is either transported to
Hell or to the river Tiber to go to Purgatory. The perfect for-
mative blood of the soul's father acts upon it like the sun's
rays on water vapor to make a rainbow creating the immate-
rial image of the soul's internal state.

Their entrance to the realm of **lust** transformed on the

seventh cornice is greeted with fire and song. As the lusty souls race through a passage of fire, they sing, "summae Deus clementiae," "God of supreme clemency". When this hymn is completed, they chant: "virum non cognosco," "I know not a man" (the words spoken by Mary at the Annunciation) and a praise for ancient **Diana**'s chastity.

Canto XXVI

When Dante's shadow falls upon the flames, the lustful, like those that came before, demand an explanation. Dante concedes to their wishes, noticing a second group running in the opposite direction shouting about "Sodom and Gomorrah" while the first group informs us of naughty **Pasiphae**'s erotic hankering for the bull. Surprise, surprise, the group numero uno is guilty of heterosexual crimes, while the counter has done the sodomite deeds.

Dante's interpreter of things lustful is Guido Guinizelli, the founder of the recently mentioned sweet new school of poetry. Dante and Guido awkwardly praise each other, but cannot embrace through the flames. Before Guido returns to the race, he introduces one even better than himself: **Arnault Daniel**. Arnault was the greatest of the troubadours, from whom all the subsequent schools of romance poetry sprang, and possibly a little too remembered for his "love" verses. Because of his importance and his loyalty to his own vernacular, Arnault speaks in Provençal. He plainly states his case and honestly asks Dante's remembrance.

IT'S JUST TOO DARN HOT...

Canto XXVII

Night has fallen. A barrier of fire blocks the only way out. Dante flinches. Virgil coaxes, "see, my son, between you and Beatrice is this wall". The three pass through. A voice sings, "Venite benedicti patris mei", "Come ye blessed of my father". The voice is that of an angel so bright that Dante is unable to see it. The three fall, exhausted, Dante with the ardours of the last P erased from his brow.

Dante dreams of Old Testament **Leah** and her sister, **Rachel**. Leah with her active life, is busily weaving her garlands of praise. Rachel, the contemplative, is gazing into the mirror of her soul.

Dante awakens to find his master already up. Virgil tells Dante that, "the sweet fruit which mortals hunger for shall this day quench you". He further explains that, by reason, he has brought Dante to this point but by emotion and instinct shall he go further. Another guide is coming, she who summoned Virgil. Meanwhile, the old Roman states that Dante has now become master of himself "body and soul". Although Virgil stays a little longer, he speaks no more.

TODAY YOU ARE A MAN—OR AS MUCH A MAN AS I CAN MAKE YOU.

I GUESS IT'S TIME TO WAKE UP AND SMELL THE AMBROSIA

126

Canto XXVIII

For the first time, Dante leads, and it's into the garden, the Earthly Paradise right at the tip-top of Purgatory. This is the **Garden of Eden**, the home of our forbears, **Adam** and **Eve**. It is still the wondrous, primal place of creation, as well as the launching pad to Paradiso (which Statius—finally finished with purgation—is anxious to try). The three halt at the banks of the river Lethe. On its opposite shore, a woman brightly sings while tending the flowers there.

Dante seems to know **Matilda** but neglects to inform us of her story. She is the embodiment of Leah, enjoying the feast of blooms growing in abundance. Matilda is also a sort of park ranger of the place and ready to explain it's ancient origins and remarkable climate. The origins we know from Genesis, but its weather was God's further contribution to its inhabitant's ease. So high it sits above the Earth's floor that no normal storm or frost can shiver its timbers. The breeze one feels is actually the gentle swoosh of Heaven's rotating spheres. The leaves stir melodically, giving accompaniment to the birds' song. The waters bubble up without origin in rain, and form the rivers Lethe, in which one must bathe to forget one's sins, and **Eunoë**, to remember all the good one has done.

Ahhh, I wish our first mom and dad had stayed on a banana diet.

Canto XXIX

The stroll into the garden continues until it is joyously interrupted. A golden light pierces through the arching boughs. Seven candelabra are carried by seven bearers in robes of unearthly white. Rainbows stream from their dancing flames. Dante turns to Virgil for some "pinch-me" reassurance. Virgil can do naught but smile. Close on the heels of these seven muses come twenty-four elders crowned with lilies, most swaying beards. These are the twenty-four books of the Old Testament. The prophets are followed by four fantastical apocalyptic beasts, described by **Ezekial:** the lion of **Mark,** the bull of **Matthew,** the eagle of **Luke,** and **John's** lamb.

These are the four gospels in their animal forms, each with Trinitarian pairs of wings and green hope wreaths. In the center of this menagerie, a golden griffon (representing Christ) pulls a splendidly impossible chariot (the Catholic Church). Around its right wheel dance three ladies: white **faith**, green **hope**, and red **charity**. At its left dance four maidens clad in regal purple: **prudence, justice, fortitude** and **temperance**. At the rear march the four elders of Christ's church, the epistoleers in white robes and red rose crowns: **James, Peter, John** and **Jude**. And at this procession's very end walks John, the author of the Revelations to be.

Thunder cannons! The pageant stops with Christ's car opposite Dante. Even Heaven loves a parade.

Canto XXX

All voices carol, "Veni sponsa de libano", "Come my bride from Lebanon", from the Song of Solomon.

A woman with an immaculate white veil held in place with a laurel wreath, clad in a green cloak, and red gown steps from behind the chariot. The figure is immediately concealed by a hundred angels raining flower petals. Dante is fit to burst with excitement. He turns to Virgil as "a child confidently seeks its mother". Virgil is gone! Not even the splendor before him can keep his eyes from spilling tears. But no, the veiled woman commands silence, "Dante do not weep for Virgil's leaving as you must first weep for other wounds".

The voice he recognizes. The veil falls. It is **Beatrice**. The angels sing for compassion, but Beatrice is not ready for that, yet. She lambastes Dante for wasting his talent, and a great treasure it is. She couldn't enlighten him in the first life, and in this she has gone down into the inferno to gain him guidance. He needs to cry for his own repentance before he can drink the waters of Lethe!

Canto XXXI

Beatrice continues her verbal chastisement of Dante. He blubbers like a baby admitting that his steps did stray from the true path when she departed the earthly plane. Not good enough for Beatrice—Dante is still not facing his transgressions like a man. At last Dante does look his sins straight in the face and he is stunned with penitence, falling to the ground in a daze.

STOP THAT BLUBBERING AND I'LL GIVE YOU SOMETHING TO CRY ABOUT.

He awakens up to his chin in the river Lethe, Matilda clutching him safe in her arms. "Asperges me," she croons ("purge me with hyssop, and I shall be clean; wash me, and I shall be whiter than snow." Psalms LI, 7). He dips his mouth into the stream and drinks.

The virtues at the shore lead him to Beatrice. They urge him to gaze into her eyes, which are fixed on the griffon's. Back and forth flows the vision of human and divine. These are truly the eyes "from which love's arrows pierced his heart".

The virtues urge Beatrice to release her veil for Dante to see her smile. She consents and, at last, Dante sees Beatrice, "in the free air heaven and earth's harmony shadows forth".

Canto XXXII

Dante is blinded by the sight of Beatrice, but only temporarily so. As he recovers, the parade moves to the center
of the garden where the tree stands. Yep, it is the tree that
started the whole human mess. It stretches upward
completely nude of leaf or flower. The griffon pulls the chariot
to its base and, with its harness, fastens it. Instantly,
leaves, blossoms and fruit spring forth. The entire heavenly
cavalcade bursts into song and Dante, enraptured, falls
blissfully asleep.

He awakens to find himself alone with Matilda, or so he thinks. No, the seven virtues are still there, as is Beatrice. They sit beneath the newly robed branches of the great tree. Beatrice announces an allegory of the "Roman" Christ for Dante to take note and relate on his return to the earthly life.

The eagle of the Roman Empire stoops to rend at the tree and chariot (the Church).

Next, the heretical fox leaps at the chariot as if at prey. Both attacks rebuffed, the eagle triumphantly returns to cover it with its wealth of feathers. Old devil dragon, by way of a fissure in the earth, rears up to damage the chariot's foundation. The battered chariot seeks protection in the remaining golden feathers, but this brings a hideous transformation—seven horned heads (the seven deadly sins) grow out from the pole and corners, four with single horns and three with double.

The monster is ridden by a corrupt and naked harlot (the bad popes). A giant consort joins her (probably **Philip the Fair** of France) and they lewdly kiss, but she has a wandering eye, and looks to Dante. Jealous, the giant beats the whore and unties the beast to drag both off into the forest.

Monster-chariot-beast, strumpet and Dante all scream.

Canto XXXIII

The virtues sing a hymn of grief for the Church. Beatrice bids Dante with Statius and Matilda to walk with her. As they walk, she makes a dire prophecy. One will come, an angry deliverer, who will destroy both whore and giant. His number shall be "five hundred and ten and five" (a reference that no one has figured out yet). Now even Beatrice can see her prognostication is a bit obscure and Dante is quite befuddled. She urges him to remember and record it accurately and, hmmm, a drink might clear his head.

Up come the virtues, who lead him to a spring, the source of the twin streams, the Lethe and Eunoë. He has drunk from the former and forgotten sin, and now tastes the latter, and all the good in him is strengthened:

> **"Born again, as a tree in spring green
> reborn; ready, to mount to the stars."**

The Paradiso

Canto I

Dante stands purified and to relate this coming supreme adventure, he must call upon not only the Muses but the divine **Apollo**, himself. He gazes upon Beatrice to see her staring, against doctor's orders, straight into the heart of the sun. It is high noon, when the sun is at its brightest. Dante follows with his eyes. For the first time Dante truly sees, "the glory of him who all things move penetrating the universe with more light here and there less".

Filled with this light, Dante perceives a second sun, a sun of spirit, and with this recognition he returns his gaze to Beatrice, the embodiment of God's love and truth, and feels himself transformed. The poet and his love rise upward, ears filled with the music of the spheres, through the sphere of fire. Needless to say, Dante is shocked at his weightlessness and sudden freedom from the tyrannous pull of gravity. Before a word is said, Beatrice explains that he must forget the laws of fleshy existence, for they are solely under the governance of the spiritual, and the gravity of the spirit dictates that all things move irresistibly toward their maker. Well, not quite irresistibly, for the souls in Hell, like a flame burning downward, have perverted the natural process.

Canto II

Let us get our bearings before we fly too high. Paradise is made up of nine heavens, each consistent with a particular celestial object. Imagine Earth as the center enclosed within these nine transparent nesting globes of Heaven outside of which lies the realm of pure godliness, the **Empyrean**, conceived as a rose of glowing souls, so the map of the universe looks like this:

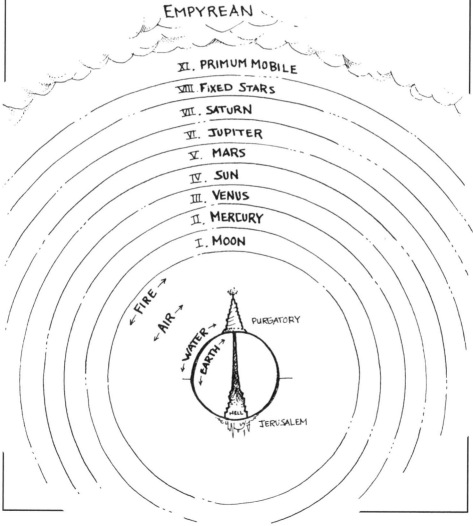

EMPYREAN

XI. PRIMUM MOBILE

VIII. FIXED STARS

VII. SATURN

VI. JUPITER

V. MARS

IV. SUN

III. VENUS

II. MERCURY

I. MOON

FIRE →

AIR →

WATER →

EARTH →

PURGATORY

HELL

JERUSALEM

One enters each heaven as soon as one has a conception of it as Dante notices their instantaneous penetration of the moon's surface. Naively, Dante asks if the moon's mottled appearance in the night sky, as he earlier postulated in the *Convivo*, is because some parts of its surface are denser, while others are thinner and thus more transparent? No way, Beatrice responds. If that were so, light would punch through the holes during an eclipse. She continues with an ingenious (and oops, incorrect) scientific experiment involving reflected light until she gets to the crux of the matter. God, this deity of energy, instructs his angels to move all matter in the universe. Each angel, according to God's commandment, does his job differently. Thus, the heavenly bodies shine, "like the living pupil of the eye," with the happiness of its place in the great scheme of things. No wonder the moon, with its position in the first heaven, shines with not quite an undiluted light.

Canto III

Dante, bathed in light, can't make heads or tails of this strange world. He turns to Beatrice, who smiles and once again cautions against using his senses like he's accustomed to on Earth. At this, Dante can at last ascertain the surrounding souls.

One soul desires speech and, at Dante's attention, spills forth with her story. She is none other than **Piccarda Donati**, sister to Dante's friend in Purgatory, Forese, and Dante's enemy in Hell, Corso. Sweet Piccarda has led an exemplary life, and certainly has no complaint about her abode in the lunar paradise. In fact, she breathes a simple invocation to God's will that ends with the prayer, "en la sua volontade e nostra pace", "in his will is our peace". But she resides in this lowest of the spheres because she was promised as a bride of Christ, a nun, and was instead married to a fellow of less divine origin, albeit against her will. Once promised, forever marked. Piccarda is joined by **Empress Constance**, who endured a similar predicament. As they sing the Ave Maria, the souls fade into the haze of illumination as quickly and mysteriously as they emerged from it.

WHEN THEY SAY NUN THEY MEAN NONE.

Canto IV

Dante is confused. If these sainted women were forced from the convent into married life, why are they assigned to the lowest place in Heaven? Beatrice informs that their true estate is in the **Empyrean**, and they only appear in the inconstant Moon, and do not fully reside there. In fact, all nine heavens have various attributes that correspond to the symbolic representations of their planets. So **Plato** (and, hence, astrology) must be correct in saying that the souls "emerge" from a particular planet and return there.

No! That is heresy and no mistake; free will is the law of God, and not the assignations of the spheres. Not to confuse the small case "will" of man for the large case "WILL" of God, humans can freely will error, but God is ever and without doubt correct.

Hmmm. Much for Dante to ponder and further question. "So can later works make up for vows broken?" Beatrice smiles with a love of such force that the poet feels weak in the knees.

Canto V

I SWEAR AND GOD MEANS IT.

What was that brilliance? Nothing less than God's light shone through, one who has given her self up to His will, which leads to a thorough explanation of vows. When one vows to the religious life, it is a pact with God and not the Church to submit to the unaltering path of Divine Grace. To break such a vow is to exert our will against Divine Will. Now, hold on.

Dante was a great advocate of the sacred outside of the monastery walls, and here with Beatrice's speech, strengthens the sacredness of all vows taken with grace. In fact, one must be very careful making any vow, for its utterance may indeed repre- sent the same compact with God as clerical orders. The Church weakens our notion of this oath-taking by its willy-nilly dispensations.

And so to the second sphere, that of **Mercury**, the planet almost invisible before the sun's rays, they commence. This is the symbolic residence of those who were good for their own honor. But good is, after all, still good. And they are gra- ciously greeted by a beaming soul.

HONOR IS GOOD, BUT ORNERY IS BETTER.

GO WEST, IMPERIALLY SPEAKING, YOUNG MAN!

Canto VI

The beamer is none other than the great Roman Emperor, **Justinian**, the Lawgiver. In contrast to the sublime shades of the Moon, his is an energetic and spriteful soul (Dante compares these mercurial folk to the darting fish in clear water). Justinian explains how he came to the purple in error, believing only in Christ's divinity and not in His humanity. Disabused of this notion by the good pope, **Agapetus**, the Emperor set himself to his grand purpose: the Law. Rome was ever the representative of true law, even in the old pagan time of Julius and his ancestors.

Constantine, the first Christian Caesar, had made the mistake of moving the seat of the Empire from Rome to Byzantium for, from the time of Aeneas, the natural place of power had moved west. And the true power was in law and the peace of justice. Occasionally wars must be fought, but only rightly in the cause of law.

Justinian continues with a chastisement of both Guelph and Ghibelline in trying to place either Pontiff's or Emperor's crown above the other because they represent God's co-equal rulers in the world of flesh. When man gets this order correct, peace will reign. At last, he finishes with a testimonial to the Provençal, **Romeo**, who though only a councilor to **King Raymond**—and an exiled one at that—still represented the holy gift of law in the land.

Canto VII

Justinian and the host of souls bid adieu with a magnificent hymn, but poor Dante is left in dismay. His noggin is in a spin over justice and vengeance, redemption and punishment. Huh? Before the question is uttered, Beatrice responds. Adam and Eve were truly made of the stuff of God, but (and this is a big but) because of their sin, their children (as well as all other animal and vegetative matter) are actually made of the stuff of angels. Not a bad thing, being made by this "second cause", but certainly a restriction on getting into Heaven. So Jesus, Mr. Divine and Human, needs to come along and redeem, and once again open the pathway to Heaven, to make us God stuff again.

Now that we are once again offered the choice, and this choice was put forward by Christ's painful and glorious re-birth from man to God on the Cross, we must, if we fail to choose wisely, suffer the full punishment for our sins. The Jews of Jerusalem were punished not for Christ's Crucifixion but rather for their refusal to see and follow his divine path. Not to follow is never to rejoin our rightful place with God in Heaven, returned always and forever to bodies made of unalloyed God stuff. Whew!

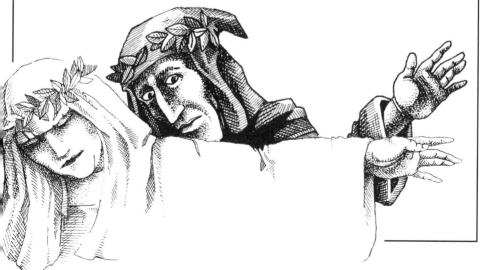

Canto VIII

Instantaneously, Beatrice and Dante are transported to the sphere of **Venus**, the last of the spheres touched by the influence of Earth, and what a touch, the touch of love. A choir of souls come forth from the Empyrean to greet them with their joyously resplendent, "Hosanna". These souls are the companions of the **Seraphim**, the most loving of all God's many bands of angels.

Love, love, love is the word, the whirl of these amorous souls. And, but for the grace of God, we might find them in lower climes if carnality had not been checked by such loving grace. One bright shining face comes forward. It is Dante's old chum **Charles Martel of Anjou**, a prince who would have been King of more than Sicily and Naples if the plague had not turned his throne into dust. Dante, ever the curious, wonders why good kings give birth to bad sons, a subject Charles is familiar with, as his bro, **Robert**, is such an unsuitable ruler. Charles sure ain't talkin' Darwin here, when he explains heredity and diversity.

See, God's big plan is that everybody has a particular thing to be. That thing is determined by matter, and matter is moved by the stars, parentage be damned. Now if you are born a swineherd, and your natural aptitude is for kingship, you got a problem. Better be king of the pigs. Dems are da breaks, and one needs to freely find one's way in the world, as difficult as that may be. Who said life was easy?

Canto IX

Oops. Chuck the Hammer (that is what Martel means) has gone on a bit, and he jumps back to continue his song and dance. **Cunizza of Romana** steps out of the chorus line to tell her tale of sinful forbears and error giving forth to light and introduces a particularly good singer, the troubadour poet, **Folco**, to carry on with his explanations.

Folco hailed from Marseilles, a port city with all the sins of a port city to bear. Folco the Rhymer had been a happy sinner there, with sins of love to rival some of the ancient myths. Eventually he transformed his love into the cowl and habit of a Cistercian monk and eventually became Bishop of Toulouse (he played a major part in the crusade against the aforementioned Albigensians). Instead of decrying his earlier transgressions, Folco sees them as the ignominious map to salvation. One thing that does get his goat, as he points out **Rahab**, the prostitute who got Joshua's spies inside the walls of Jericho, is Christendom's (read Pope's here) failure to get some good Christians inside the wall of Jerusalem.

Go figure.

SHE ISN'T JUST A CLICHÉ — SHE WOULDN'T BE HERE WITHOUT A HEART OF GOLD.

Canto X

On to the fourth heaven, the sphere of the **sun**. Dante pauses to take note of God, that trinity of Creator, wise son, and loving spirit, and his ineffably subtle creation, the universe. The genius of the rotating spheres is in its imperfect perfection. The small tilt of the Earth's axis arranges seasons and diversity. In that diversity is the rich and complicated love of the Creator for his Creation. And there is the circular love of God for himself.

Dante is startled from his prayer by a luminous halo of twelve spirits crowning both him and Beatrice. These are the twelve doctors of the Church, the unflagging suns of ecclesiastical wisdom. **St. Thomas Aquinas** is their spokesman and in short order, introduces the other eleven: **Albert Magnus**, Thomas' contemporary of Cologne; **Gratian**, who brought civil and canon law into accord; **Peter Lombardus**, whose theological writings became the Church's textbook; **Solomon**, the Old Testament smarty pants; **Dionysius**, the man who discerned the orders of angels; **Orosius**, a fifth-century historian; **Boethius**, whose *Consolation of Philosophy* was one of Dante's greatest influences; **Isidore of Seville**, who consolidated early medieval learning in his *Cyclopedia*; the venerable **Bede**, who wrote extensively of both Church and English history; **Richard of St. Victor**, a twelfth-century Scottish mystic and anti-rationalist and **Siger De Brabant,** a follower of the Muslim philosopher, Averroes, who was considered by Aquinas a heretic, but Dante thought him to be a great champion of the unpopular opinion, who was made to suffer for it. Quite the distinguished group!

IF YOU ONLY HAVE A HEART, A BRAIN, THE NOIVE . . .

Canto XI

St. Thomas senses some questions in Dante's mind, which certainly must be an open book to these exalted folk, and proceeds to explain. The Church, God's true bride on Earth, has been blessed with two unequaled proponents of man's dual path to God: the heart and mind, love and knowledge. **St. Dominic** and his order, the **Dominicans** of which St. Thomas is a proud member, pursue learning as **St. Francis** and his brethren rejoice in the spirit of the Seraphim.

Thomas graciously remembers Francis to his company. Divinely inspired, Francis embraced poverty as his bedmate and hand in hand with her gathered a company distinguished for their good works. His evangelism took him all the way to the Sultan, and if **Saladin** didn't exactly convert to Christianity, he at least became more tolerant of it. At the end of his arduous life, Francis was visited by God's love in the form of the Stigmata and peacefully expired a poor saint in a mountain cave. Would that contemporary Dominicans follow Frank's penurious example instead of wedding greed.

Canto XII

As St. Thomas finishes his speech, a second crown of twelve souls becomes apparent and a voice, soon introduced as **St. Bonaventure**, takes its turn at the podium, this time in praise of **St. Dominic**. Dominic was a tireless laborer in the acquisition and distribution of God's truth. His special mission was to the Albigensians and, failing to convert them, heauthorized their destruction. Dominic's truth was not a warm and fuzzy one.

Bonaventure decries the falsehood that his Franciscan brothers have fallen into, graciously giving tat for tit with Thomas. He introduces the eleven other bright spirits, a less distinguished band but containing a few brilliant lights like **St. John Chrysotom**, "The Golden Tongue" of Byzantium and **Joachim of Fiore**, the Mystic and Prophet.

> OKAY, WE'RE B-LIST SAINTS, BUT THIS IS STILL HEAVEN.

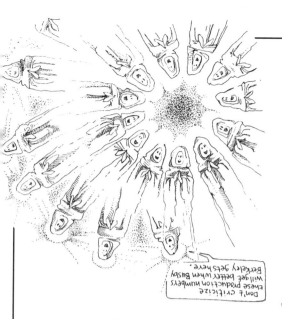

Don't criticize
these production numbers
will get better when Busby
Berkeley gets here.

Canto XIII

The twenty-four spirits arrayed in two concentric rings around Dante and Beatrice begin a stately dance. One circle moves in one direction and the second spins in the other direction, forming two wheels of light whirling in the ether. They hymn a paean to the Trinity and the two natures of Christ, divine and human.

As awestruck as Dante is, he is ever the questing intellectual, and the simple question of the heavenly dispersion of wisdom comes to mind: if Adam ate of the fruit and Christ was the Son, how is it that Solomon is the smartest? St. Thomas, mind reader that he is, responds before the curl of a lip, or a slip of the tongue. Everyone, through inspiration, heredity and environment, is equipped with differing talents. This is only half the story, however, for a talent is only worth its weight if you grow and use it. So, **King Solomon** is the supreme example of the person who doesn't hide his talent under a bushel basket. He invests and spends and reinvests until his is a whole granary full of talent. Such was his interest and his job. And you, Mr. Smarty Pants Dan, should sidle up to your judgments like an old man with a walker instead of doing a Greg Louganis right in.

Canto XIV

Still Dante has more questions. The radiance of the saints is no small thing and Dante "whats?" at its wattage. Like a power surge, the souls spin and sing their praise again, and a voice enters Dante as a stone causes ripples in water. It is **Solomon**, and his response comes even before Dante can form another question.

> YOU KNOW YOU CAN'T JUST TAKE A SWORD AND SEPARATE BODY FROM SOUL.

The true substance of humanity is both soul and body. Heaven encompasses the completeness of creation, hence all that Dante sees will, at the Last Judgment, have not only a physical presence, but a glorified one. That's why we will have that certain glow and the ever-ready energy to sing and dance through eternity.

Another halo of light forms and Dante is startled to find that he and Beatrice both have risen to the fifth sphere, the heaven of **Mars**. A vision of the Cross pierces the sky, and amidst his bedazzlement, Dante meets Beatrice's gaze, "The holy beauty of those eyes becomes more pure as we rise".

Canto XV

Dante is almost at the point where an unglorified body can take no more of this exquisite pleasure: Beatrice. The warrior saints form a brilliant cross in the Martian sky, they sing their rapturous song, which quiets, and from which a single shooting star of a soul comes plunging to face the over-whelmed. "Speak aloud," the spirit wishes, for the human voice has its own sweet music. Dante concedes and inquires the presence's name. It is **Caccigida Alighieri**, Dante's great-great-great grandpa, and as codgers are wont to do, he talks about Florence in the good old days.

"Yep, you shoulda seen it then. Simple, not all the geegaws and folderol people parade about with these days. Geez, you could even see what the ladies looked like not all disguised with paint. It was the kinda place that could inspire a lad like myself to go crusading with the Emperor Conrad and get knighted, too. 'Course I did come home on my shield, but that got me here as a martyr."

Canto XVI

Well, Dante is just about to bust his buttons when Beatrice chills him with an indulgent smile. "More, more, tell me more," Dante still insists. And old Cacciguida complies.

"Quite the place our little Florence, but then all this Guelph and Ghibelline nonsense started. Pope shoulda kept his nose outta politics. And then it really hit the fan when the **Buondelmonte** family moved into the neighborhood. Already we had the **Gualterotti** and **Importuni** bunches stirring the pot, but when Mister Buondelmonte broke his marriage word to Ms. Amidei, sheesh, the bloodshed was like Florence was sacrificing to old Idol Mars himself again."

FLORENTINE WHIPPERSNAPPERS! FIGHTIN' AMONGST 'EMSELVES WILL GIVE WAR A BAD NAME!

Canto XVII

Dante hears the sad history of his home and this puts in mind some of the dark hints he picked up in the *Inferno* and *Purgatorio* about his own fate. Beatrice urges him to ask. He does. Cacciaguida answers after a preamble on prophecy and free will. Seems if will was truly free, nobody would have a chance of even guessing what would happen next? Not so. Will is indeed free—it is our conception of time that is lacking. We living folks sense it as a linear progression while those heavenly eternals get the whole picture. Time as a unity—past, present and future are one! Don't worry, you'll understand it once you step through Peter's gates.

Dante gets the straight poop about what life has in store (remember, he set the book in 1300, although he began writing it in 1306 and finished in 1321). And boy did he step in it. Thankless politics, faithless friends, exile. Dante will know how "hard it is to taste the salt of another's bread". Hope will rise only to be lost with **Henry VII**, but don't envy the crowd that plays patsy and keeps their butts in the cushy chairs. When they have become dust, people will honor the memory of Dante.

I GOT SOME GOOD NEWS AND SOME BAD NEWS— FLORENCE IS GONNA BE REAL NICE TO YOU AFTER YOU DIE, BUT WHILE YOU'RE ALIVE . . .

BUT I'M STILL ALIVE AREN'T I ?

Canto XVIII

Dante takes this augury with some bitterness. It is a hard thing to learn that you will spend a great deal of your life depending on the kindness of strangers. Beatrice cheers him with, "Remember, I am ever in the presence of he who rights all wrongs". Dante perks up and Cacciaguida introduces some of his companions: **Charlemagne** and his peer, **Orlando**, the man with the horn; **Godfrey of Bouillon** and **Robert Guidcard**, the former a leader of the First Crusade and the latter a founder of the crusading **House of Tancred**, as well as a battler who sacked Rome and had Pope Gregory picking up his skirts to flee. Grandpa rejoins the illustrious company and the hymns ring out again.

Dante gazes at Beatrice. Her beauty grows. He realizes they are ascending to the sixth sphere, the sphere of **Jupiter**. From its silvery globe, the singing souls, like some heavenly marching band, form the opening words of Solomon's Book of Wisdom: "Diligite justitiam; Oui judicatis terram",

> IT'S A BIRD! IT'S A PLANE!

> No! IT'S THE SOULS OF THE JUST RULERS!

"Love justice. You who judge on Earth". As they watch more souls fly out from the terminal "m" expanding into a great eagle of empire entwined with the lilies of France.

Such a magnificent display of the symbols of justice fill Dante with a sadness at how astray the realms of Earth have wandered under a corrupting papal rule.

Canto XIX

For the moment, Dante is dumbstruck as the eagle, composed of all the just and righteous rulers, begins to speak with one voice. But he is speechless only for a moment, and in the next, asks a question that has perplexed him all the way from Hell's first circle, "Why are the just pagans confined to limbo?" The eagle explains that finer minds than his have fielded such questions. Even the light bringer, **Lucifer**, questioned, and because he could not understand the reason of God, rebelled in confusion. There are more things under Heaven and Earth than humans are given to understand. But don't despair, at the Last Judgment those good pagans will find themselves closer to Christ than many who have called his name.

GEEZ, a talkin' bird

That's the good news. The bad news is that many contemporary kings and potentates that hold their seats under the will of Heaven are so incredibly unworthy.

From the farflung regions of Hungary to Portugal, from tongue twisters like Rascia and Nicosia and Famagosta, Christian rulers are making a right rum job of it.

Canto XX

The eagle ceases speaking as one, and the many voices chime like thousands of gentle bells flowing into a murmur not unlike the song of a rushing stream. This hum moves into the eagle's throat, and once again, it speaks. The eye of the bird is made up of the six noblest leaders of them all. The Old Testament contributes such as the pupil **David**, distinguished in his own right, but also Christ's fleshy antecedent and **Hezekiah**, the King of Judah, whose justice won him a reprieve of death for fifteen years to carry on the good work. **Constantine the Great** is there, even though he moved Christ's capital from Rome to Byzantium, but he gets points for Christianizing the Empire, and the more contemporary **William of Sicily**, the last of Guiscard's House of Tancred. The other two inhabitants of the eagle's eye shock Dante. The first is the Old Trojan, **Ripheus**, and the second is the Roman Emperor, **Trajan**. Both were, by all accounts, pagan. In fact, Ripheus lived hundreds of years before Christ!

You might say—
WE RULE!

Dante blurts, "Che cose son queste?", "How can this be?" The eagle patiently explains that not everything in Heaven can be discerned by the mortal mind, but maybe this can help: Ripheus was converted by a vision of Christ. In a sense, he was so just that he could anticipate the establishment of Christianity, and Trajan was actually returned from Limbo to his body long enough to convert.

Dante is overjoyed. This revelation offers hopes of redemption for all those grand shades in Limbo, and especially for his beloved mentor, Virgil. Hooray!

Canto XXI

Beatrice and Dante ascend to the seventh heaven, the sphere of **Saturn**. Dante looks to Beatrice for her ever-brightening smile. She does not smile. Her smile has grown so impossibly bright that Dante would instantly be consumed and turned to ash "as was Semele" when seeing the full glory of Jupiter were he but to glimpse it. That's divine dentistry for you.

Saturn is a golden crystal orb with a Jacob's Ladder of purest gold stretching upward from its surface. All seems silent, but Dante's ears are as yet unable to discern the rarified music. As they watch myriad splendid souls descend the ladder, only one comes down all the way to greet them. Even before a suitable introduction, Dante is Mr. Questions. The spirit is quick to respond. Predestination is one of those subjects that isn't exactly for God to know and for you to find out. Lotsa stuff you never find out.

The spirit is **Peter Damiano**, who called himself Peter Peccator, "Peter the Sinner" to you. Peter lived in a tumbledown monastery in Fonte Avellana and remained in his humble circumstances even after he graduated to wear the Cardinal's red. Peter is unhappy with the current state of greed in the Church. He gets the other contemplatives—for this is the Heaven of the meditator—creating such a mighty din that poor Dante's mortal ears go into complete collapse.

Canto XXII

The perturbed spirits had formed a circle around our travelers to let loose their noise and from this round the most radiant of all comes to poor Dante, who is being calmed by Beatrice. This brightest spark is good **St. Benedict**, founder of the Benedictines and author of the Rule of Orders, by which every Monastic organization abides. Benedict assures Dante that any question is okay, even the unanswerable ones. Dante asks Ben to appear in all his glory. Benedict replies that you have to go higher to see that, all the way to the Empyrean, where all of one's desires are fulfilled.

As ever, the sinners and saints put in their comments on the contemporary situation, Benedict displays the empty Jacob's Ladder that spans from Saturn down, conspicuous by its emptiness. Recruits in the Holy Orders are not fit to put foot to rung. But hey, there is hope, and with a tornado spin, all the souls whirl back up the ladder.

BEATRICE, I CAN SEE YOUR HOUSE FROM UP HERE.

Beatrice raises Dante upward to his birth constellation, Gemini, in the eighth heaven of the fixed stars. As they fly, she urges Dante to remember his journey in these heavens, and relate them in words for all to read. She pushes his gaze downward from whence he came. Down through all the seven spheres, he spies the Earth. Like those later astronauts, he ponders its beauty and fragility in the vast expanse of space. Such a tiny place to generate such endless cycles of war and suffering.

Canto XXIII

Beatrice indicates the region of Summer Solstice, the constellation of Cancer. His eyes brim with a rushing flood of light. Christ is its crest. Too much, too much, this vision. Dante's mind is blasted.

He comes to, able again to behold Beatrice in her glory, and from her, back to the light. **Jesus** has ascended to the Primum Mobile. The Rose of Motherhood, **Mary**, is summoned upward by her Son. Her flame flies to His presence.

The radiance of the lilied Apostles and the cavalcade of saints pulse tenderly up to bathe and touch the Savior and His Mam.

Dante picks out the keys' first keeper, **Peter**, in the rapt throng.

DON'T TELL ME—
IT'S LIKE "E=mc²"
OR SOMETHING.

Canto XXIV

Beatrice appeals to the glorious
company of the sanctified to
share with Dante a morsel of
their feast of ecstasy. Dante is
indeed a hungry man, and he
has come a long way for a meal.
St. Peter comes forth and,
always the toll-taker, proposes
a small test. Dante is put in
mind of his college days in Bologna
and is ready for his orals.

Peter inquires, "What is faith?"

Dante answers, "Faith is the substance of
what we wish to see and the argument for what is unseen.
This, it seems to me, is its essence."

Peter: "Correct, but why first this substance and then
this argument?"

Dante: "What exists here in Heaven is unseen by mortal
eyes. Its substance is believed, not seen. Its argument is
our belief without visible proof."

Peter: "Do you believe?"

Dante: "Like a fresh minted coin that is ever bright and
unworn."

Peter: "Where does this faith come from?"

Dante: "The Holy Spirits' rain of unending gold."

Peter: "But why do you believe this is divine in origin?"

Dante: "Because I can see the works that follow from it."

Peter: "How do you know of the existence of such works?"

Dante: "Faith flowed through the world and made it Christian, not miracles."

All the assembled saints sing, "Te Deum Laudamus", "God We Praise".

Peter: "Very good, but what is it you believe?"

Dante: "I believe in one God, sole and eternal, loved and desired by creation, the unmoved mover of all the worlds. The truth of his existence comes not only from Moses and all the prophets, but from the testimony of my senses. I believe in the Trinity in whose being is Eternity. The spark of belief has raged into flame and like a star illuminates my being."

Peter smiles and the host circles Dante singing joyous praise.

I DON'T CARE IF BALTIMORE HASN'T BEEN FOUNDED YET— YOU STILL HAVE TO KNOW YOUR CATECHISM!

SO WHAT AM I? CHOPPED LIVER?

Canto XXV

But the test is not over. The Apostle **James** takes the podium to quiz the poet on hope.

James: "That you are called to experience and write while still alive will stir up hope and love there below. Do you have hope?"

Dante: "No one in the Church has greater."

James: "What is hope?"

Dante: "Hope is the sure expectation of a future glory. It is the fruit of divine grace."

James: "What does hope hold out to you?"

Dante: "The scriptures are the signposts pointing to God's promise. All God has chosen are blessed."

James cries: "O Lord, let them hope in thee!"

A light brighter than all of the others comes forth and Dante is dazzled to blindness. It is **John,** he who lay on Christ's breast (referred to as the "Old Pelican" in this passage because of the medieval belief that this bird so loved its young that it nourished them on its own blood).

HOPE IS THE ROPE YOU HANG ON TO NOT THE ROPE THAT HANGS YOU.

Canto XXVI

Dante is assured that Beatrice will restore his sight when the time is right. Dante declares Beatrice is the gate for that greater love that Alpha and Omega of scripture testify. John is pretty darned impressed, and begins the test on Love.

John: "So, what set your bow at this lofty target?"

Dante: "Philosophy, spiritual authority. Good itself kindles love for the greater good. Everything yearns for the loves of its first cause and first love."

John: "So reason and writ urge you; anything else?"

Dante: "The sacrifice on the Cross offers love irrefutable!"

"Holy! Holy! Holy!" The heaven's ring and Dante's eyes open to the inconceivable (and indescribable) beauty of Beatrice. He passes with truly flying colors.

A fourth flame approaches, the soul of everybody's dad, **Adam**. Time for Dante to set his journalist's cap once again.

Adam wasn't given the bum's rush out of the Garden for eating the fruit 4302 years before the Jubilee (1300). He was persona non grata because he disobeyed God's orders. Adam lived to the ripe age of 930, old enough to see Babel rise and fall, and when he finally died, he went to Limbo to await the harrowing on Holy Saturday.

LOVE DOES MAKE THE WORLD GO ROUND.

SO DON'T SIT UNDER THE APPLE TREE WITH ANYONE ELSE BUT ME.

Canto XXVII

Peter returns, and quite literally sees red. His eyes and very spirit glow with passion at the sad state that office he founded has fallen into. He rails and spews at the papacy and its larcenous corruption. The tears and blood shed from **Linus** to **Cletus** to **Sixtus** on down to **Urban** only to be dirtied by the likes of **Clement** and **John** and the worst of all, **Boni-face VIII**! Peter's righteous fury tints the very heavens red.

The saint finishes his diatribe with a command to Dante to write of the foul depravity of the modern papacy. Inquiring minds need to know and change it. The last words said, the souls in contravention to the Law of Gravity, but in keeping with the laws of divine nature, fall upwards to the highest heaven like drops of flame.

Dante and Beatrice, growing even more impossibly beautiful, follow suit and ascend to the ninth heaven, the **Primum Mobile**. This is the heaven ultimately encased in the supreme will of God representing the works that turn the sum of nature. From this lofty height, a small jewel not quite basking in the sun's full illumination floats pregnant with the spring of goodness Beatrice predicts will come soon.

Canto XXVIII

Dante sees a curious sight mirrored in Beatrice's eyes. He turns to take it in fully. Around a point of purest light whirl nine concentric rings. Beatrice explains, "from that point hangs all heaven and nature". Indeed, the point is God, and the spinning wheels are the orders of angels.

Dante is confused. God is all embracing, but also the center? The angels in the closest rings, the **Seraphim** and **Cherubim**, are also the ones whose abodes are furthest flung in the heavens? Beatrice calms Dante with a theory of relativity, by which all is explained but still mysterious. The angels who are purest in their love for God sweep closest to his heart and the closer they are, the farther the reach of their cleansing wings.

The traveler and his companion can hear the sweet three-part harmony of the angels' "Hosanah". Three-part because they are divided into three trinities of praise. The first is made up of the Seraphim and Cherubim, joined by the **Thrones**. The second trio is comprised of **Dominations**, **Virtues**, and **Powers**. The final go-rounds are the **Principalities**, the **Archangels** and lastly, the ordinary, everyday, happy **angels**.

167

Canto XXIX

It is time for Beatrice to answer all the unasked questions: what, when, where, how? In the fathomless reaches of eternity (time exists only for the created), God perceived the reflection of his abiding light. Suffused with love, the joy of "I am", he transformed the reflection into a universe filled with the same capacity for love. Potential and act were one and the same—there was no separation. The angels were born at the time of all creation.

Beatrice cautions against all the false extant teaching. Even **St. Jerome** fell into some confusion as to time and circumstance of God's creation. Many are there who spin fables and split hairs without even the germ of truth. Beware the folly of even good intentions. Truth, like the primal light of God, is truth.

SO MY PAL, JER, HAS A PROBLEM WITH TIME — WHERE'S THE LOVE?

Canto XXX

As dawn brightens the sky and the stars are submerged in an all encompassing light, so the Primum Mobile and all the universe are consumed in God's reflected river of light as Beatrice and Dante enter the **Empyrean**.

The Empyrean, beyond time and space, is the true abode of God. Dante has been slowly prepared for its revelation. At last, he sees Beatrice in all her transfigured glory. At last, he can look upon all the souls of the blessed surrounding and rapturing God's bright center like petals of a mystic rose.

Canto XXXI

Angels wing forth and back like bees going about their fertilizing work. Forth and back from God the center to the furthest petals of the flower of this "sacred soldiery". Rank on rank, the sainted host, passionate and peaceful, sit in joyous contemplation of the Trinity.

Dante turns to Beatrice. She is gone, and in her stead is old **St. Bernard** (not a bad choice for a scout). Bernard points to Beatrice in her rightful place in the Heaven flower: the third row down from Mary the Mother, and just to the left of biblical Rachel, Eve sits in the row between Mary and Rachel.

Beatrice meets Dante's eyes. Love flows and Dante realizes that the love he has for her is the love he has for God. And God was ever the guide.

Bernard, famed Cistercian monk and dedicated follower of the B.V.M. (Blessed Virgin Mary) signals to the Holy Mother's throne with sweet devotion. Dante is finally able to raise his eyes to the glory. All is gladness.

Canto XXXII

Bernard, never taking his eyes from the Virgin, explains the seating of this vast amphitheater of the blessed. In its center is the depthless lake of light, the illumination of God washing over all the saints and reflecting throughout all creation.

The rose itself is divided into two categories of the redeemed. on the right sit those who died before Christ's coming and on the left those who died after. Bernard identifies many in the configuration, saints old and new. The whole shebang appears something like this:

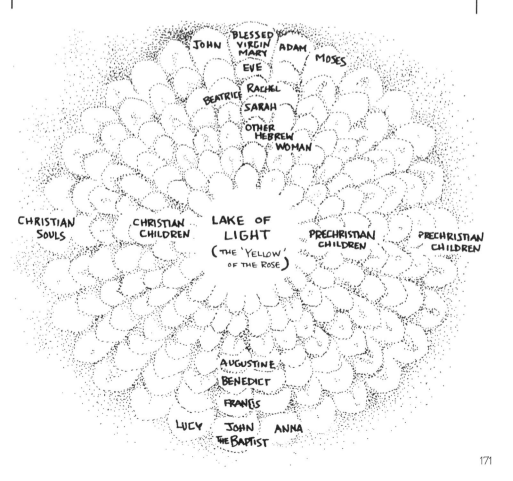

The ranks of the pre-Christians are filled to capacity. The Christians, on the other hand, have plenty of space to fill. Remember: the geometry of Heaven is such that those who appear furthest are actually nearest, so Mary is one and at the same time the outside rim and the closest to the center.

Bernard, his tour finished, begins a prayer.

Canto XXXIII

It is a prayer to Christ's immaculate mother, an entreaty to she who helps all who ask, and many who don't, "for he who has come from the universe's deepest pit, upward through the

soul's three realms/I pray you allow this final vision, the joy supreme…"

As it is prayed, Dante can see without looking. No words dare describe the ultimate sight that all creation longs to see, the sight of God in all His glory, in all His love.

Dante tries to describe what he has seen, and what he has every hope of returning to in the future. There within the center of the rose, in the lake of light, he sees the final unapproachable mystery: three circles of light, but one only. The second reflected rainbow cast by the first and the third a fire breathed by the first two. Words can do no justice in touching the phenomenon of this living tripartite ray.

Further smitten by our own likeness being reflected in this eternal light, Dante admits his failure of imagination, even as his desire and will are rolled like a wheel, perfectly balanced, moved "by the love that moves the sun and other stars".

L'amor che cove il sole l'altre stelle.

he great work Dante had begun, possibly as early as 1306, was finally completed in 1321. The poet had been staying with **Guido Novello** in Ravenna, and had undertaken an embassy to Venice for this kind patron in August.

Venice in summer lets slip its disguise to reveal the pestilent swamp on which it is constructed and its virulence visited Dante. He returned with fever to Ravenna.

On 13 September, Dante, who had been there and done that, set out to do it all again.

He was buried in the Church of St. Francis.

Nel gallo de la rosa sempiterna,
che' dove Dio sanzo mezzo governa,
odor di lode al Sol che sempre verna ...

lines 124-126
Canto XXX
PARADISO

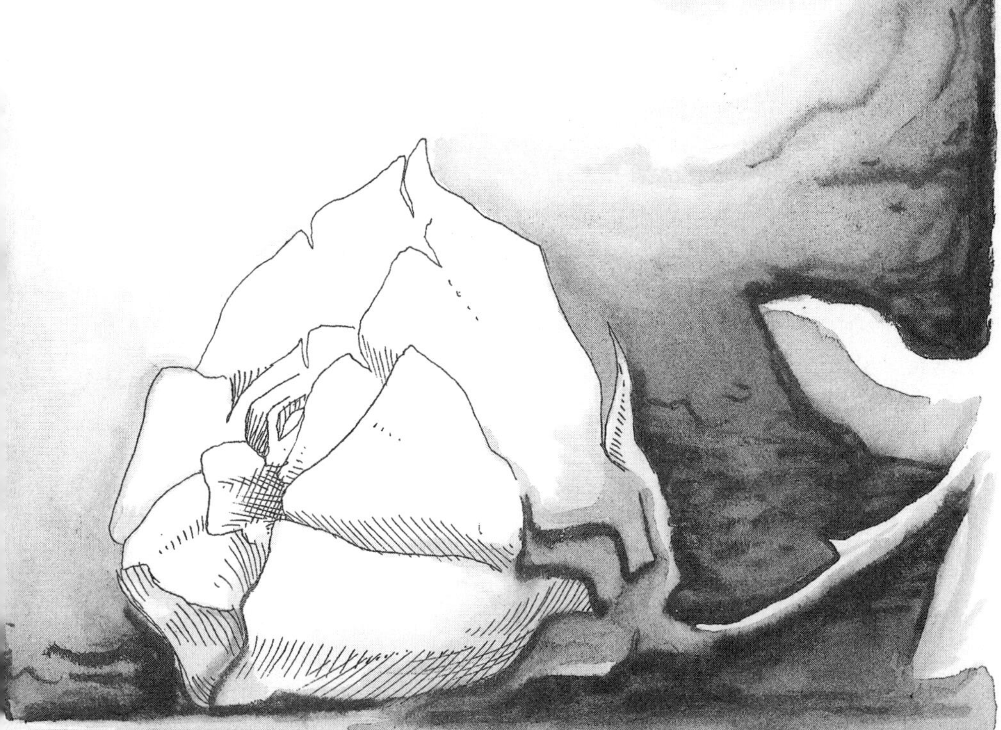

Bibliography

References

Anderson, William, *Dante The Maker*, The Crossroad Publishing Co.,
    New York, 1982

Brandeis, Irma, *The Ladder of Vision*, Anchor Book, New York, 1962

Chubb, Thomas Caldecott, *Dante and His World*, Little, Brown and
    Company, Boston, 1966

DeGennaro, Angelo A., *Dante's Divine Company*, Philosophical Li-
    brary, Inc., New York, 1986

Gilbert, Allan, *Dante and His Comedy*, New York University Press,
    New York, 1963

Jacoff, Rachel, (Ed) *The Cambridge Companion to Dante*, Cam-
    bridge University Press, New York, 1993

Kirkpatrick, Robin, *Dante: The Divine Comedy*, Cambridge University
    Press, New York, 1987

Luke, Helen M., *Dark Wood to White Rose*, Parabola Books, New
    York, 1989

Rossetti, Maria F., *A Shadow of Dante*, Little, Brown and Company,
    Boston, 1900

Williams, Charles, *The Figure of Beatrice*, The NoonDay Press, New
    York, 1961

Translations

Carlye-Wicksteed, *The Divine Comedy*, Modern Library, New York, 1950

Cary, Rev. Francis, *The Divine Comedy*, Chartwell Books, 1984. Illustrated by Gustave Doré.

Ciardi, John, *Divine Comedy*, W.W. Norton and Company, Inc., New York, 1977

Mandelbaum, Allen, *Divine Comedy*, 3 volumes, Bantam Books, Inc., 1980, 1982, 1984. Illustrated by Barry Moser.

Musa, Mark, *Divine Comedy*, 3 volumes, Indiana University Press, Bloomington, 1971. Illustrated by Richard M. Powers.

Phillips, Tom, *Dante's Inferno*, Thames and Hudson Ltd., London, 1985. Illustrated by Tom Phillips.

Rossetti, Dante Gabriel, *Dante's Vita Nuova*, George Routledge & Sons, Ltd. Illustrated by Dante Gabriel Rossetti.

Schneider, Herbert W., *De Monarchia*, The Liberal Arts Press, New York, 1949

Sinclair, John D., *The Divine Comedy*, 3 volumes, Oxford University Press, New York, 1961

Wicksteed, Philip H., *Dante's Convivio*, J.M. Dent & Sons Ltd., London, 1903

The Author

Joe Lee is an illustrator, cartoonist, writer and clown. A graduate of Ringling Brothers, Barnum and Bailey's Clown College, he worked for many years as a circus clown. He is the author and illustrator of Writers and Readers' **The History of Clowns for Beginners®** , and the illustrator of the Jung, Postmodernism, Shakespeare and Eastern Philosophy titles in the same series. Joe lives in Bloomington, Indiana with his wife, Mary Bess, three cats and Toby, the fox terror.

accept no substitute!

> Great ideas and great thinkers can be thrilling. They can also be intimidating.

That's where **Writers and Readers *For Beginners*** books come in. **Writers and Readers** brought you the *very first For Beginners* book over twenty years ago. Since then, amidst a growing number of imitators, we've published some 80 titles (ranging from Architecture to Zen and Einstein to Elvis) in the internationally acclaimed *For Beginners* series. Every book in the series serves one purpose: to UNintimidate and UNcomplicate the works of the great thinkers. Knowledge is too important to be confined to the experts.

And knowledge, as you will discover in our **Documentary Comic Books,** is fun! Each book is painstakingly researched, humorously written and illustrated in whatever style best suits the subject at hand. That's where **Writers and Readers For Beginners** books began! Remember if it doesn't say...

Writers and Readers ®

...it's not an original *For Beginners* book.

**IRIS MURDOCH
FOR BEGINNERS®**
Bran Nicol
Illustrated by Piero
ISBN 0-86316-401-3

US $11.95
UK £7.99

Iris Murdoch was famous for writing some of the most interesting fiction of the twentieth century: novels that are serious and 'literary', but gripping, funny, and strange, too—a kind of intellectual soap opera. But to call her a novelist tells only part of the story. She was also an eminent philosopher, respected literary critic, sometime playwright, poet, librettist, Dame of the British Empire, Booker Prize winner, Oxford don. Some would even say she was an enchanter, an eccentric, a mystic, a saint, and one of the lovers in 'the love story of our age'...
Iris Murdoch For Beginners® provides an entertaining introduction to this extraordinary writer. It explains the power of novels like *Under the Net, The Bell* and *The Black Prince*, but it also shows that the only way to really understand Murdoch's fiction is through the author and, expecially, the ideas behind it. So this book doesn't just assess Murdoch's achievement as a novelist and tell the story of her life, career, her sad death and its aftermath. It gives a clear and lively introduction to her philosophy—its context, influences, and main concepts. As a philosopher Murdoch took on many of the most important thinkers (like Plato and Sartre) at their own game, but never departed from her belief that philosophy should be immediately relevant to the kind of experiences each of us go through every day.

So if you've enjoyed Murdoch's novels and want to understand them better, or haven't read them but are thinking about it... If you want to know what existentialism, metaphysics, and moral philosophy are, what 'Eros' and 'ascesis' mean... If you've ever wondered where we should look for moral guidance in a world without God, if you've ever confused obsession with love... **Iris Murdoch For Beginners®** is for you.

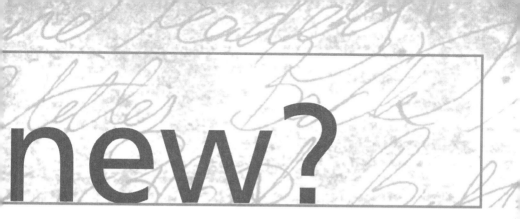

new?

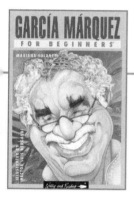

**GARCÍA MÁRQUEZ
FOR BEGINNERS®**
Mariana Solanet
Illustrated by
Héctor Luis Bergandi
ISBN 0-86316-289-4

US $11.95
UK £7.99

Nobel Prize-winner Gabriel García Márquez is Latin America's most powerful literary symbol. In three decades, his novel *One Hundred Years of Solitude* has sold over twenty million copies in more than thirty languages, to become the most famous and widely-read novel in Spanish since Cervantes' *Don Quixote*.

García Márquez For Beginners® introduces readers to the man and his 'magical realism', a style that expresses Latin American life and culture in many different layers of human perception.

Gabriel García Márquez has pledged that everything he writes comes out of the real world, including gypsies on flying carpets, a woman ascending to heaven, body and soul, and a priest who levitates when he drinks chocolate.

Throughout his career, from 'The Story of a Shipwrecked Sailor', which first brought national acclaim as a journalist, through the many novels, short stories, writings for cinema to the winning of the Nobel Prize for Literature in 1982 as well as his political and human rights activities, García Márquez has remained an intensely private individual.

This book pays an essential and illuminating visit to the life and works of the Colombian writer who has been described as 'the world's most important living writer' and who is said to represent 'the voice and the spirit of Latin America'.

**GARCÍA LORCA
FOR BEGINNERS®**
Luís Martínez Cuitiño
Illustrated by
Delia Cancela
ISBN 0-86316-290-8

US $11.95
UK £7.99

1998 marked the centenary of the birth of one of Spain's brightest stars in the fields of poetry and drama, Federico García Lorca. His poetry never goes out of print and his plays still have an impact on audiences throughout the world. Lorca or 'Federico', as he was known, was born in Granada in 1889 and was executed, without trial, at the age of thirty-eight by the Falange at the start of the Spanish Civil War.

Lorca was one of the most influential and talented members of the avant-garde movement of his generation. His chilling and compelling drama *Blood Wedding* established him as the dramatist who revived Spanish-speaking theatre.

Lorca appealed to all levels of Spanish society; he merged popular art forms such as gypsy songs and lyrics with classical poetry and music.

In **García Lorca for Beginners**®, Luís Martínez Cuitiño analyses Lorca's work within the context of his life—a life filled with passion and drama—while Delia Cancela's illustrations compliment the text by recreating the line and style of Federico's own drawings.

**RUDOLF STEINER
AND ANTHROPOSOPHY
FOR BEGINNERS®**
Lía Tummer
Illustrated by Lato
ISBN 0-86316-286-X

US $11.95
UK £7.99

At the dawn of the twentieth century Rudolf Steiner created Anthroposophy, the 'spiritual science' that opposes the blindly science-believing, materialistic ideology inherited from the previous century. In so doing, he introduced a truly humanistic concept. Based on a profound knowledge of the human being and his relationship with nature and the universe, Anthroposophy has not only been able to provide renewing impulses to the most diverse spheres of human activity, like medicine, education, agriculture, art, religion, etc., but is also capable of providing answers to the eternal questions posed by mankind, towards which the 'natural sciences' remain indifferent: what is life? where do we come from when we are born? where do we go when we die? what sense has pain and illness? why does some people's destiny seem unjust

Rudolf Steiner and Anthroposophy for Beginners® describe this universal genius' solitary growth from a childhood in the untamed beauty of the Austrian Alps to the sublimities of human wisdom.

new?

**EASTERN PHILOSOPHY
FOR BEGINNERS®**
Jim Powell
Illustrated by Joe Lee
ISBN 0-86316-282-7

US $11.95
UK £7.99

Eastern philosophy is not only an intellectual pursuit, but one that involves one's entire being. Much of it is so deeply entwined with the non-intellectual art of meditation, that the two are impossible to separate.

In this accessible survey of the major philosophies of India, China, Tibet and Japan, Jim Powell draws upon his knowledge of Sanskrit and Chinese, as well as decades of meditation. Whether tackling Buddha, Confucius, Lao Tzu, Dogen, the Dali Lama or Patanjal— Powell's insights are deeply illuminating.

All the major philosophies of India, China, Tibet and Japan are explained and the spiritual rewards and intellectual challenges of Eastern philosophy are revealed in this visually stunning book.

This is an exceptionally beautiful **For Beginners®** book, with 19th-century engravings throughout.

Everyone—from beginner to expert—will find **Eastern Philosophy for Beginners®** a beautiful and insightful overview.

**PIAGET
FOR BEGINNERS®**
Adriana Serulnikov
Illustrated by
Rodrigo Suarez
ISBN 0-86316-288-6

US $11.95
UK £7.99

Jean Piaget's theory of intellectual development is a result of his life's work, spanning almost 80 years of study. His contribution to the field of child psychology is equal to that of Sigmund Freud's achievements in psychiatry. Piaget's aim was to find the answer to the epistemological question: how do you construct human knowledge? Or: how do you acquire precision and objectivity?

Through interviews and tests with children (including his own), Piaget and his colleagues studied the acquisition and development of knowledge in the course of childhood and adolescence, from which he developed his theory of genetic psychology. His work has inspired numerous studies in the fields of education and developmental psychology.

Piaget for Beginners® investigates the key moments of the scientist's life, which are also landmarks in his own personal and professional development.

How to get original thinkers to come to your home...

Individual Orders

US
Writers and Readers Publishing, Inc.
P.O. Box 461, Village Station
New York, NY 10013
www.writersandreaders.com

UK
Writers and Readers Ltd
PO Box 29522
London N1 8FB
Phone: 020 7226 2522
Fax: 020 7359 1406
begin@writersandreaders.com
www.writersandreaders.com

Trade Orders

US
Publishers Group West
1700 Fourth St.
Berkeley, CA 94710
Phone: 800.788.3123
Fax: 510.528.9555

Canada
Publishers Group West
250 A Carlton St.
Toronto, Ontario M5A2LI
Phone: 800.747.8147

UK
Littlehampton Book Services Ltd
Faraday Close
Durrington
Worthing, West Sussex BN13 3RB
Phone: 01903 828800
Fax: 01903 828802
orders@lbsltd.co.uk

South Africa
Real Books
5 Mortlake St.
Brixton, 2092
Phone: 2711 837 0643
Fax: 2711 837 0645

Australia
Tower Books
Unit 9/19 Rodborough Rd.
French Forest NSW 2086
Phone: 02 9975 5566
Fax: 02 9975 5599

SHIP TO (NAME)

ADDRESS

CITY   STATE   ZIP

COUNTRY

TELEPHONE (DAY)   (EVENING)

To request a free catalog, check here: ☐

Title	Quantity	Amount
SUBTOTAL		
New York City residents add 8.25% sales tax		
Shipping & Handling: Add $3.50 for 1st book, $.60 for each additional book		
TOTAL PAYMENT		